OKLAHOMA HORIZONS SERIES

C.D. NORTHCUTT,
WILLIAM C. ZIEGENHAIN,
BOB BURKE

Palace on the Prairie

The Marland Family Story

Foreword by George Nigh

Series Editor: **GINI MOORE CAMPBELL** • Associate Editor: **ERIC DABNEY**

Copyright 2005, by Marland Mansion, Inc., Ponca City, Oklahoma. No reproduction of this material may be made without the written permission of Marland Mansion, Inc.

Published by Oklahoma Heritage Association, 1400 Classen Dr., Oklahoma City, Oklahoma 73106.

Printed in Canada
ISBN: 1-885596-48-0
Library of Congress Control Number: 2005934462
Book cover and contents designed by Sandi Welch/
 www.2WDesignGroup.com
Cover photography by Robert Burke
Unless otherwise noted, interior photographs are from the
 Marland Mansion Collection.

The authors are especially grateful to the *Ponca City News*, and its publisher, Tom Muchmore, far left, for preserving the history of the Marland Mansion and the Marland family. For more than 30 years, Louise Abercrombie has meticulously chronicled the relationship between the Marlands and Ponca City.

Dedication

THIS BOOK is dedicated to Paul and Maxine Prather for their years of service in researching, restoring, and preserving the Marland Estate and the history of the Marland family.

Paul Prather spent countless hours using his special skills with paint, glass, and wood to refurbish and restore furnishings. He often used his own funds to buy original pieces of furniture for display. He built a new wooden west gate and crafted the new gate at the entrance to Lydie's cottage. He used his expertise in framing to prepare the large paintings on display in the mansion and adjacent buildings.

Paul and Maxine Prather were passionate about the restoration of the Marland Estate after its purchase by the City of Ponca City in 1975. *Courtesy Ponca City News.*

Known for many years as the curator emeritus of the Marland Estate, Paul kept meticulous records of his research on the mansion and the family. He and Maxine traveled to other parts of the United States, talking to anyone who might have a Marland connection.

Paul had direct contact with Lydie Marland in her final years. He visited with her frequently before her death in 1987 to confirm the accuracy of furnishings and detail of the estate. His ongoing love for the history of the Marland Family and dedication to the preservation of the Marland Estate was unquestioned.

—The Authors

Foreword by George Nigh   7

I	A ROYAL ANCESTRY	9
II	WESTWARD TO OKLAHOMA	23
III	OIL BARON	35
IV	PRINCESS LYDIE	55
V	THE TAKEOVER	79
VI	GOVERNOR MARLAND	87
VII	THE END OF AN ERA	103
VIII	THE HOMECOMING	113
IX	RETURN TO GRANDEUR	127

The Genealogy of the Marland Family   157

Marland Family Timeline   177

Mayors of Ponca City   179

Marland Estate Directors   181

Bibliography and Suggested Reading   185

Acknowledgments   187

Index   188

Foreword

AS I WRITE THIS FOREWORD in the summer of 2005, the State of Oklahoma has started its countdown toward its Centennial. Just think, there are Oklahomans in whose lifetime is contained the entire history of their state.

And what a history it is—unduplicated in the 50 states. It is a short story with many chapters; most depending on which part of these 69,000 square miles you want to know about.

People normally relate to the places and things that shaped their lives. One of the most defining parts of my life were the years spent studying and teaching Oklahoma History, the story of all 77 counties.

While a teacher at McAlester High School, I first became enamored with the Marland Mansion. Little did I realize that another part of my later life would bring this magnificent structure off the pages of the history book. I had always read, heard, and taught about it, but did not understand the mystique of this "Palace on the Prairie" until I went there. I really was not prepared for its grandeur, its history, its glory days, its bust days, nor did I truly understand the characters who lived, played, and visited there.

C. D. Northcutt, Bill Ziegenhain, and Bob Burke cut to the chase in this intriguing story of an intriguing place. You do not have to wait as long as I did to know all about it and to be amazed at a place so near, yet so far away.

While living in the Governor's Mansion for eight years, Donna and I had or created opportunities to not only enjoy the Marland Mansion ourselves, but to host many friends and guests there.

When former President Bill Clinton was a fellow governor of Arkansas, it was our pleasure to host him there. While Jimmy Carter was President, it was our pleasure to host his mother, "Miss Lillian." The list could go on and on but it would be hard to top the list that E.W. Marland entertained there. In all cases, every guest would find it hard to believe that such a place could exist here on the prairie. But it did, and it does.

One of the most interesting chapters of its history is about Lydie Marland—it will captivate you that the former First Lady of Oklahoma, who was also the Lady of the House at the Marland Mansion, just simply disappeared for many years, and upon her return chose to live in the chauffeur's house, tend the gardens, and walk to town unnoticed.

Donna and I were hosting a formal event at the Mansion shortly after Lydie had returned to Ponca City. Donna thought it appropriate that Lydie be invited so she sent her two dozens red roses with an invitation to join us. Lydie sent back a long hand note expressing her regrets and graciously declined the invitation. Then she noted the beauty of the thought as well as the roses, kept one in appreciation, but returned the remaining flowers for everyone to enjoy.

I hope this book increases your interest to not only know the lore and history of the Marland Mansion but make you want to visit the estate in person. You will be glad you did.

—George Nigh
Former Governor of Oklahoma

and large amounts of cotton were discarded as a result. Alfred put this observation into his memory for the time when he could develop a sturdier strap. That idea would have to wait, however, until he had facilities to put his plans into a working model.

In 1868, Alfred married Sarah McLeod Smith, a widow with five children. Sarah was born October 12, 1836, in Dundee, Scotland, the first of three children of David and Margaret McCloud. Family stories said David served in the military on the Isle of Skye during her early years and that her education began there.

In 1855, Sarah married Henry Smith, a blacksmith. While living in England, Sarah gave birth to her first child, a daughter, Sarah Anne Smith. Sarah Anne would later have a son, Franklin Rockefeler Kenney, who would be instrumental in bringing E. W. Marland to Ponca City, Oklahoma.

Between 1858 and 1866, Sarah gave birth to twins, David Henry and Jane Elizabeth, and two other children, Margaret Jane, and William John Baily Smith. It is believed that Henry Smith died in 1867. The following year is when Alfred met the widow Smith and began his courtship for her

ABOVE: A copy of the marriage license of E.W. Marland's paternal grandparents, George and Anne Whitworth Marland. They were married at Oldham Church in Lancashire, England, in August, 1836. *Courtesy Richard Myers.*

BELOW: The Marland family coat of arms adorns the end of a pew in an Episcopal church in Rochdale, England. The church dates from A.D. 637. *Courtesy Richard Myers.*

A Royal Ancestry

ERNEST WHITWORTH MARLAND had the bloodline of a true English gentleman. For centuries, his ancestors were landowners in Lancashire, England, in the town of Ashton-Under-Line, a suburb of Manchester.

On Marland's father's side, records of the Church of England list one of Marland's ancestors, Alfred Marland, as the donor of a stained glass window in the Rochedale Parish church in Lancashire in the 15th century, about the time Christopher Columbus was discovering America.

In the same English church yard cemetery are the graves of Marland's grandmother's family, the Whitworths. Marland was named for his maternal great, great grandfather, Ernest Whitworth, considered by men of letters of his day as one of the great mathematicians in England. Whitworth owned and ran the private Whitworth School for Boys at Ashton-Under-Line, the same village which sent Marland's father, Alfred Marland, off to the Crimean War at age 15. When injured in the battle of Balakva, Alfred was cared for by a young nurse, Florence Nightingale, who gave him a small, leather-bound Bible she inscribed, "To my beloved friend, Alfred Marland."

On his return to Lancashire, Alfred sat under the teaching of his famous grandfather until he, himself, became a teacher of mathematics and English. Soon, however, the lure of the New World drew him across the Atlantic Ocean. In 1862, Alfred, as an engineer and master mechanic, emigrated to America and worked in the Philadelphia shipyards on the battleships of the day. Like many Englishmen, he sided with the South in the Civil War. He joined the Confederate Army for a short time.

Shortly after the Civil War ended in 1865, and Alfred's employment in the construction of battleships for the Union navy was no longer needed, he moved to Pittsburgh, Pennsylvania, to work in the steel industry. The industry was experiencing rapid growth because of the growing need for steel for railroads moving west and for reconstruction following the war. Alfred found early employment on a riverboat and noticed how much waste was involved in the shipment of cotton bales. The bindings on the bales would loosen during their handling

PHOTO BY ROBERT BURKE

No doubt the list of guests that have been entertained at the Marland Estate is impressive. Mike Mott and Jayne Detten portray E.W. and Lydie Marland in the formal dining room. Courtesy M.A. Crank.

LEFT: Alfred Marland, E.W. Marland's father, was born in 1837 in Ashton-Under-Lyne, Lancashire, England and died in Ponca City, Oklahoma, in 1914. *Courtesy Richard Myers.*

ABOVE: Richard Myers, a distant cousin of E.W. Marland, stands with a Marland family headstone in the Mt. Lebanon Cemetery in Pittsburgh, Pennsylvania. *Courtesy Richard Myers.*

hand. He treated her children as his own, and looked forward to making a life with her.

Alfred and Sarah began their family together with the birth of Charlotte Ann, called Lottie on December 10, 1869, followed by another daughter, Ignatia, called Natia, born on November 4, 1871. Finally, Sarah gave birth to a son on May 8, 1874. He was christened Ernest Whitworth Marland. All three Marland children were born in Pittsburgh.

The 1870 Pittsburgh city directory lists Alfred as a machinist living at 1214 Virgin Alley. He acquired machine tools necessary to make a cotton baling strap. And, after several attempts, he was successful and was able to sell his idea to earn money for badly needed capital.

In 1874, Alfred's residence is listed as Southern Avenue, Ward 32, in southern Pittsburgh. He was still listed in the city directory as a machinist until 1882, when his designation changed to "mill boss." In 1883, he was part-owner of the Marland, Neely Nut and Bolt Company on South 21st Street in the steel district.

Gradually, Alfred became a rich man. He was elected to the state legislature from South

BELOW: E.W. Marland's older sister, Charlotte Anne "Lottie" Marland, was born in Pittsburgh, Pennsylvania in 1869 and died in Ponca City in 1927.

RIGHT: E.W. Marland's second sister, Ignatia M. Marland, was born in Pittsburgh in 1871 and died in 1951 in New York, New York. Her second husband was rubber company president Louis K. Rittenhouse. He was murdered during a much-publicized hold-up attempt in front of his New Jersey home in 1924.

Hills and later served 20 years on the Select Council of Pittsburgh. On five select acres in South Hills, on Mount Washington, Alfred built a 12-room home surrounded by a vineyard, flower gardens, stables, and barns. Historian John Joseph Mathews wrote, "He would live as a gentleman ought to live; he would create an unpretentious manor here in the beautiful hills of Pennsylvania."

Young Ernest was raised in a lifestyle of culture and learning, recognizing the importance of the English first-born male. The Mount Washington home had a large library that contained the best of literature. Alfred, using his

BELOW: James Marland, an uncle of E.W. Marland, was born in England in 1861 and died in Washington, Pennsylvania, in 1955. James was only 4 feet eight inches tall. *Courtesy Richard Myers.*

E.W. Marland's uncle, Henry Marland, and his wife, Elizabeth "Lizzie" Marland. Henry was born in England in 1841 and died in 1934 in Wilmington, Delaware. *Courtesy Richard Myers.*

A ROYAL ANCESTRY   13

A current photograph of the house at 131 Southern Avenue in Pittsburgh, Pennsylvania, where E.W. Marland spent his childhood. In 2005, the home was still being used as a residence. *Courtesy Richard Myers.*

teacher's instincts, instructed his children to read at the earliest age possible, with the best diction and posture. Alfred often told his son that an English gentleman had responsibilities to society, that "of him to whom much is given, much is required."

Ernest was a leader, even as a child. When he played with neighbor children, he made up rules for games. He was bright and filled with dreams, some no doubt fueled by the stories he read from books in his father's library, although he was known to make up stories of which he was the hero or the leader.

Ernest was not an athlete—his short legs were not conducive to winning foot races. He also was not a leader because of any superior mental capacity. Instead, he became a leader because, with his vivid imagination, he convinced those around him that he knew what he was talking about. Young Ernest proved his self-assurance by winning game after game of "keeps" marbles. He greatly enjoyed showing off his winnings by carrying a huge sack of marbles he had won from neighborhood boys.

Ernest was prolific at writing poetry and making up fairy tales. At the dinner table he heard names of the great industrialists of the time—John D. Rockefeller and J. Pierpont Morgan, although those names were icons of his father's generation and did not necessarily impress Ernest.

Alfred's home in Mount Washington was a meeting place for many cultured people of Pennsylvania. The latest social and political ideas were discussed in the parlor. A foreign visitor was Sir Thomas Hughes, a noted liberal author who came to America to establish a colony where the children of Englishmen who were tired of intensified industrialization could be educated in the freedom of the American frontier.

Hughes established the colony in 1879 in the Cumberland Mountains of Tennessee. He built a church, a town hall, and other community buildings from native pine. Hughes called his town Rugby, and his educational experiment, the Arnold School, named for the headmaster of Rugby School in England, the scene of Hughes' novel, *Tom Brown's School Days*.

Alfred visited Rugby and was so impressed with the pristine surroundings and the Spartan discipline of Hughes' school, he gave money for the project and decided to send Ernest to board and learn there. Ernest always remembered his first morning at Rugby. He ran to the window of the inn and saw 50 to 100 men on horseback, garbed in red coats and ready to start on a fox hunt. The scene made a deep impression upon him, allowing him to introduce fox hunting to Oklahoma a half century later.

At Rugby, Ernest was the only American-born boy among the 50 students. He learned much more about being an English gentleman than what he digested in the classroom. He hunted foxes and played tennis. His father generously contributed money and ideas to Arnold School. A self-described "chubby little fellow," Ernest learned Latin from a birch stick-wielding Reverend Blalock and read the classics. When his family visited, they stayed in Ivey Cottage at Rugby, a house built and paid for by Alfred.

Ernest's mother spent most summers at Rugby, although Ernest was allowed to return home for Easter and Christmas.

Soon, however, Hughes' colony began to fail because of the lack of labor to work the farms. Seeing the demise of the school, Albert pulled Ernest from the colony.

Back in Pittsburgh, Ernest first attended public schools where some of the sons of mill workers taunted him. His boxing training at Rugby allowed Ernest to win most of the scraps in which he was involved.

When Ernest was 14, he was enrolled at Pittsburgh's Park Institute, a private school from which he graduated at age 17 in 1891. As a teenager, Ernest began questioning his father's teaching that money alone does not make a gentleman. He was fascinated by ladies with parasols riding in carriages pulled by high-stepping horses. He was in awe of businessmen who dressed in the latest fashion and spent their afternoons smoking cigars with their friends in bars. Ernest was impressed with rich people, especially Henry Clay Frick, the very rich king of the coke mills of Pittsburgh, and Andrew Carnegie. Before he was 18, Ernest told his friends he wanted to be a businessman and to be very rich.

Ernest entered law school at the University of Michigan in 1891. Two years later, his father, devastated by the panic of 1893, suffered financial losses and was forced to sell his interest in the business to his partner. After selling the Mount Washington home, Alfred and Sarah moved to rural Hancock County, West Virginia.

Ernest lived with 20 young men in the Sigma Chi fraternity house on the campus of the University of Michigan in Ann Arbor. At 17, he was the youngest member of his law school class. He wore high-starched collars, bowties, and a derby hat. When not in class, he enjoyed socializing with his fraternity brothers with much beer-drinking and poker-playing.

Poker reminded Ernest of playing "keeps" marbles. He loved to gamble, a trait that certainly benefited him later in life in the oil business and politics. At law school, possibly because of his tender age, he was not in a leadership role. He did not take part in social activities but did play as a substitute on the school's baseball and football teams. In fact, the onetime leader of childhood games in the world around Mount Washington became self-sufficient and silent. One of his fraternity brothers described him as "a good looking chap with good color, although his features were somewhat on the coarse, sensual order, with rather heavy eyes, sometimes almost sleepy, that might have given to the casual observer an impression of indolence."

Living in a fraternity house was not the plush existence to which Ernest was accustomed. The Sigma Chi house was a rented cottage on East Huron Street that had only one bathing facility—a tub made of sheet metal that was heated by three Bunsen burners.

Ernest was not a great student—but he was an excellent poker player. He did not distinguish himself to his professors but did graduate from the Michigan Law School in June, 1893. His father had lost much of his real estate holdings because of an economic downturn that had severely affected the industrial-based economy of Pittsburgh. All Alfred had left was his home and surrounding property in nearby West Virginia.

Without a job, Ernest moved into the home of his sister, Ignatia. His father could not provide him with living expenses or a job, but did recommend him to an attorney, Kirk Q. Bigham. Ernest was only 19, two years younger than the age required to be admitted to practice law in Pennsylvania. Therefore, all Ernest was allowed to do was to assist lawyers in preparation of cases and in representation of clients. Ernest earned $10 a week, the first money he ever made on his own.

Bigham had a substantial law practice and Ernest was busy, running down information from clients and witnesses who lived in the poorer sections of Pittsburgh. For the first time, he was introduced to the other side of society, the coal-dust-covered faces of miners and the weathered hands of steel mill workers. On any day, he dealt with the poorest or richest that Pittsburgh had to offer.

Even though he was so young, Ernest was afraid of being insignificant in the world, of being an outsider looking in on the wealth and power of Pittsburgh. When he was 21, he was admitted to practice law in the state of Pennsylvania. Bigham was planning retirement and informed Ernest he would be closing the law office.

Rather than join another law firm, Ernest opened his own law office on Diamond Street, in a small space under a stairwell. Ernest's sister was his secretary and his father gave him money to pay rent. His main clients were James M. Guffey and John H. Galey, coal promoters, for whom he inspected potential land for strip mining, examined titles, and crafted contracts. Even though Ernest was officially a lawyer, he sincerely did not think that he could ever make much money as a lawyer but intended to use his law degree to somehow vault him into big money.

Even when Ernest, now called E.W. by his associates, was not turning a profit, he was nevertheless spending money like a successful lawyer. He spent afternoons lifting a champagne glass in local bars, winding yarns of his schemes for making money. One scheme was hatched as E.W. rode a streetcar to work each morning. Advertising cards placed between the roof and windows of the car were dull and uninviting. In the privacy of his room, E.W. developed colorful cards that were less stiff and caught the attention of riders. With his profit from selling the cards, E.W. looked for some new business in which to make the big money of which he dreamed.

In 1895, as E.W. was opening his own law office, he came upon an opportunity to get into the oil business. For the previous four years, oil production in Pennsylvania had substantially dropped due to a national financial panic. But as E.W.'s interest turned toward oil, the price went to $2.70 a barrel. Speculators crowded Pittsburgh's Oil Exchange. Bankers were lenient with their loans to wildcatters who worked over older wells that had become unprofitable and were temporarily shut-in during the panic. With

LEFT: Mary Virginia Collins married E.W. Marland in Philadelphia, Pennsylvania, on November 5, 1903.

a few dollars he had saved, E.W. purchased an occasional oil interest.

For the time being, however, E.W.'s life still revolved around coal. He believed in his ability to put together successful purchases of coal mining leases. He promoted such ventures as the West Virginia Coal Company, as he moved his attention to coal fields in nearby states. When Guffey and Galey's money could not finance his dreams, he turned to the main bank in Pittsburgh founded by Judge Thomas Mellon. Loans from the Mellon Bank allowed E.W. to dream bigger and expand his operations into more fertile coal fields. E.W. was general counsel of one of the promotion companies headed by banker Andrew Mellon and broker George I. Whitney.

In 1901, E.W. became general counsel and president of the Pittsburgh Securities and Guaranty Company, founded to join investors with coal mining speculators in Pennsylvania and West Virginia. But oil was his future. He later recalled "the memorable day" in 1898 when an oil interest in West Virginia's Turkey Foot oil field became productive and he began receiving royalties. The oil bug had bitten E.W. in a huge way.

During his travels, E.W. began spending more time with Mary Virginia Collins who was working as a court stenographer in Philadelphia. Mary Virginia, the second of five children of Samuel C. and Lydie "Eliza" Miller Collins, was born in Philadelphia on July 7, 1876. Collins served in the Pennsylvania legislature with E.W.'s father. E.W. spent many hours smoking expensive cigars with Collins at Steele's bar in Philadelphia. The two had first met when, as a promoter, E.W. was spending time in the state capital of Harrisburg where Collins was clerk of the Superior Court of Pennsylvania.

Collins was a first generation American of his family that had emigrated from Ireland. His father, Thomas, was born in 1810 in Ireland and came to the United States as a young man looking for a future. He married Jane Price who gave birth to three sons and a daughter. Samuel was born in Philadelphia in 1850 and was influential in the city's politics. He was educated and often quoted poetry during his visits with E.W.

After months of courtship, E.W. and Mary Virginia were married in a quiet ceremony in the Collins' home in Philadelphia on November 5, 1903.

E.W. became a self-taught geologist. In investigating coal fields for investors, he learned from engineers and surveyors about how veins of coal were discovered. To correctly evaluate a potential coal field he had to be able to identify coal formations and outcroppings of sandstone. He learned from oil drillers that the distance between the Pittsburgh coal veins and the Mahoning sandstone was always the same, whether their oil wells were five miles apart or 100 miles apart, or on top of a hill or in a deep valley. He soon could predict the presence of the first oil sand beneath the sandstone.

As one of the first men to use geology to locate oil successfully, E.W. noticed a potential source of oil while surveying for coal in Hancock County, Virginia. After obtaining leases from a half dozen farmers in the area, he hired a drilling contractor and sank a well in the spring of 1905. However, at age 31, E.W.'s first oil well was a dry hole.

Convinced that he was right in picking that particular place to drill a well, E.W. bought his drilling partner's interest and kept drilling. E.W.'s persistence paid off. The very next well hit gas, and then oil, and caught on fire. The oil ran down a creek and into the Ohio River for 20 to 30 miles. People spotted the oil stains and followed the colored hue upstream to E.W.'s well. Excitement about the gusher spread like wildfire.

Oil men came in swarms. E.W. remembered, "That was the wildest place you ever saw. The oil men jumped in and grabbed everything they could." They called it the Congo field, after the name of a nearby railroad station. E.W. drilled 54 more wells in the field without a dry hole. All wells were producers, from 500 to 1,000 barrels a day.

From the Congo field came E.W.'s first big money. Production from the 55 wells made him his first million dollars. He turned down offers from Standard Oil Company to take the wells off his hands and use their pipeline to get natural gas to market. Instead, he built his own pipeline under the Ohio River into East Liverpool, Ohio, where there awaited huge pottery plants looking for an inexpensive fuel source.

RIGHT: Samuel C. Collins, Jr., Mary Virginia Marland's brother, worked with E.W. Marland in oil ventures in both West Virginia and Oklahoma. He later became vice president of the Marland Refining Company.

Samuel C. Collins, Jr., was born in Philadelphia, Pennsylvania. His early business activities were as a member of the Philadelphia Rapid Transit Company. Later he became associated with Mr. Marland in the production of oil in West Virginia. Mr. Collins has been connected with the Marland Companies since they were first organized. He is now Vice-President of Marland Refining Company and Director of Marland Oil Company in Charge of Marketing.

RIGHT: Mary Virginia Marland, left, and her brother, Samuel Collins, Jr., at a picnic along the Ohio River in 1906. They were celebrating the successful completion of a gas well.

E.W. was making $2,500 a day from selling gas to the potteries. Then, on November 1, 1907, another financial panic struck the nation. Banks suspended cash payments. E.W. kept huge sums of money in five different Pittsburgh banks that went broke. For 18 months the potteries remained closed. Because of the panic, E.W.'s incredible success in the oil and gas business suddenly turned sour. Once again, he was broke.

He was 34 years old and still owned a huge house he had built with money from the Congo field. However, with hundreds of thousands of dollars in unpaid bills, he and Virginia stored their furniture and moved back to Pittsburgh. He and friends drank a lot during the time of depression at the old Henry Hotel.

Like ice in August, his fortune had been swept away. What he retained however, was his excellent reputation in the industry for knowing where to drill for oil. In discussions with other oilies, he heard about new oil fields "way out west" where he had never been—in Oklahoma, of all places.

RIGHT: Mary Virginia Marland, left, and E.W. Marland's aunt, Anna Eliza Sperring. Her husband was James Marland, brother to E.W.'s father, Alfred Marland. *Courtesy Richard Myers.*

ABOVE: E.W. and Mary Virginia Marland in West Virginia in 1907. Soon after the photograph was taken, a financial panic devastated his fortune, and E.W. looked toward the frontier in Oklahoma as the next place to look for oil.

A ROYAL ANCESTRY

II

Westward to Oklahoma

E.W.'S ABILITY as an independent contractor interested oil companies in Pittsburgh that had operations in Kansas and Arkansas. He almost went to work for one of the companies, but the president of the company would not meet his demand for $750 a month.

He may have been broke, but E.W. kept up his appearance. He bought a new house in the Squirrel Hill section of Pittsburgh, but soon lost it also. He kept a new silk hat he wore as he attempted to clean up his financial affairs. To end the financial nightmare, he deeded his properties to his principal creditor, Oil Well Supply Company. He told John Eaton, the head of the company he was heading west, to Oklahoma, or perhaps to California. Eaton, who liked E.W., gave him a letter of credit that could be used at any Oil Well Supply house in the west. The letter would be invaluable later.

E.W. had heard of oil strikes at Red Fork and Glenn Pool in Oklahoma. He was chomping at the bit, even desperate, to be on the ground floor, to be part of the passion and wealth of the age just over the horizon—the age of oil. He told his friend, Gene Waldo, that Oklahoma was one of the last few remaining frontiers in America, "an unplumbed land of possibly great potential." So much oil had been found so quickly by so few that the enormity of the resource might be unimaginable. "Oklahoma," E.W. said, "not the East, was the place to be."

E.W. left Pennsylvania with railroad fare, Eaton's letter of credit, and enough money to pay his board for a month or two. While visiting relatives in Chicago, Illinois, he talked with his nephew, Lieutenant Franklin Rockefeller Kenney, who had been stationed in Oklahoma where he became friends with rancher George Miller.

Miller and his two brothers had inherited a large ranch they called the Miller Brothers' 101 Ranch. The huge spread had become famous for its Wild West show and raising cattle and grain crops.

E.W. and Kenney set out for Oklahoma to meet Miller with the idea of convincing the ranch owner to lease his lands for oil drilling. The Miller brothers controlled more than 100,000 acres and ran their operations from a large home known as the "White House," six miles south of Ponca City.

BELOW: Franklin Rockefeller Kenney, E.W. Marland's nephew, was assigned as an Army officer in Oklahoma at the turn of the twentieth century. Kenney told his uncle about the 101 Ranch, the Miller Brothers, and the potential for oil and gas in the region.

The ranch was located in a rectangular strip of land covering six million acres along the Oklahoma-Kansas border, a tract originally identified as the Cherokee Outlet because the Cherokees had been granted the right to use the land as a passage from their reservation in Indian Territory to hunting grounds in southeast Colorado. In 1893, the six million acres, now called the Cherokee Strip, was opened for qualified settlement.

Located in the eastern portion of the Strip, west of the Osage Nation, were reservations of other Indian tribes who had been moved into Indian Territory. All these tribes, except for the Ponca and Kaw, had sold their surplus lands to the government. The surplus lands were also opened for settlement in the run of September, 1893.

E.W. arrived in Oklahoma in December, 1908, only a year after Oklahoma became the 46th state of the union. He stepped off a train without fanfare at the Santa Fe depot in Ponca. E.W.'s coming to Oklahoma would change the course of many lives. John Joseph Mathews painted E.W.'s first impression of Oklahoma and Ponca:

There were no mountains or river gorges to claim E.W.'s attention when he descended from his coach; there were only the sky, a few buildings, and a few surprisingly fine residences. To one from Pittsburgh, the little cattle and wheat town seemed somnolent and the people passively inquisitive in their casual glances. The little town lay shining in the sun, unprotected from nature's tantrums. It was a geometrical figure, cross hatched with monotonously straight streets which terminated suddenly in a limitless plain of close-growing grass, yellow or tawny with the autumnal change or emerald green like a carpet when the winter wheat had sprouted. To the east, however, the streets stopped abruptly at the edge of the Arkansas River flood plain.

Immediately south of the little town was the Ponca Indian Reservation, where the Salt Fork of the Arkansas cut the plain with its cottonwood and elm and its tangle of vines and thickets. Dotting the plain were the small houses of the Ponca, with their brush-covered structures close by.

Robert E. "Bob" Clark, Jr., whose father was later one of E.W.'s treasurers, described E.W.'s entrance to Ponca:

His premonitions told him oil would be found under the uncharted rolling prairies of northern Oklahoma, and he had come to Ponca City to find it. His entrée to the Miller family, he believed, had been more than fortuitous; with his luck it was meant to be. Always he had an unshakeable confidence in his luck, his belief that he could succeed where others had failed; and now having arrived in Ponca City he was impatient to get started. He would get in touch with the Millers.

He would give Lady Luck a whirl around the floor. As he stood on the station platform, the smell of oil, unrecognizable to the rank

LEFT: A poster advertising the Wild West Show of the 101 Ranch. Included are the photographs of the three Miller brothers who founded the ranch. *Courtesy Oklahoma Historical Society.*

and file, was in the air—musty, penetrating, unmistakable, an aroma that made the heart beat faster, the senses quicken. In West Virginia, he had first picked up the smell, a bewitching, addictive scent whose track now led him to Oklahoma, a land alive with possibilities, yet free of undue restraint.

Even more importantly, the Oklahoma outback was far from the gluttonous clutches of the money barons and monopolistic cartels. The barons and cartels would be here in time, but for now, he was free to explore this virgin territory, having time enough to perhaps gain a significant foothold in an industry already appropriated in the East by Standard Oil and its fellow conspirators, John D. Rockefeller, Andrew Mellon, and J.P. Morgan. Merchants of greed he called them. They were expropriators, not explorers, he liked to say, hyenas who confiscated the spoils after the lion had made the kill.

Ponca City's history is rich. Months before the Cherokee Strip was opened for settlement in 1893, B.S. Barnes traveled present-day Kay County looking for a good place to build a new town on the frontier. He found a spring near the B & M ford across the Arkansas River. The ford was on a well-traveled wagon road that stretched from Kansas to Osage country.

Knowing that a good water source was a necessity for any successful town, Barnes logged the legal description around the area of the spring and went back to Arkansas City, Kansas, and organized the Ponca Townsite Company. On

LEFT: The Arcade Hotel was the first home of E.W. and Mary Virginia Marland in Ponca City. *Courtesy Ponca City News.*

Downtown Ponca City, looking East from First Street and Grand Avenue, in May, 1896. *Courtesy Ponca City News.*

September 21, 1893, four days after the land run that opened the Cherokee Strip, Barnes' surveyors completed their division of the town site into lots.

Interested settlers began drawing for lots. A small girl drew cards from a box placed on present Grand Avenue between Third and Fourth streets. Pioneers paid $2 each for a certificate that gave them title to either a business or residential lot. More than 2,300 certificates were sold and recorded in large bound books. This is believed to be the first time a new city was founded in America with a drawing for lots. Ponca City was born after two days of drawings.

The city went through several name changes in its first two decades of existence. First known as New Ponca, the post office changed its official name to Ponca on July 7, 1898, two years after the post office at the nearby Ponca Indian Agency had changed its name to Whiteagle.

At Oklahoma statehood in 1907, Ponca became part of Kay County. The county had originally been designed as county "K." On October 23, 1913, the United States Post Office

ABOVE: Mary Virginia Marland holds a baby fox outside the Arcade Hotel where the Marlands lived when they first arrived in Ponca City.

RIGHT: E.W. Marland at the wheel of his new touring car outside the Arcade Hotel in Ponca City.

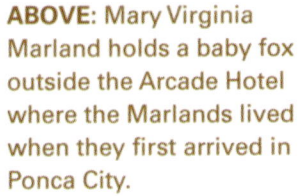

Mary Virginia Marland, standing at center of photograph, takes a glass of punch during a party in the dining room at Ponca City's Arcade Hotel. *Courtesy Ponca City News.*

Department officially changed the town's name to Ponca City.

E.W. made the Arcade Hotel, on the southwest corner of First Street and Grand Avenue, his home in Ponca. The hotel's beginning was in the township of Cross, since absorbed by Ponca City, as a frame building owned by G.W. Light. After the building was moved to Ponca in the late 1890s, it became the town's leading lodging place and was built onto twice, partly with brick. By the time E.W. arrived, the hotel had already been visited by presidents, cowboys, and many guests to the 101 Ranch. Later, the hotel's most famous occupant was oil man and philanthropist Lew Wentz who lived in an apartment at the Arcade for 38 years.

E.W. liked his first impression of Ponca. Bob Clark wrote, "The streets were alive with buggies and a few automobiles, the stores appeared to be well stocked, and a few substantial homes flanked Grand Avenue. On his way to the Arcade Hotel with his bags, E.W. paused to read two notices posted on a bulletin board along a dirt sidewalk. One notice told of a dance scheduled for Saturday night at Barnes Hall. The other poster announced a prayer meeting on Sunday morning at the First Baptist Church—sinners were especially welcome. E.W. chuckled to himself, 'Dancing and sinning. You can't do one without being the other.'

For three days, E.W. rode a rented buckboard around Kay County, surveying the area's topography, billiard table flatlands to the west, rolling, anticlinal hills to the east, and splicing between lay the meandering Arkansas River valley with its silty alluvial plan and fractured limestone rim out of which oil had oozed here and there for a millennia."

Gazing over the land, he sensed oil was beneath it, perhaps in huge quantities that would boggle the mind. Bob Clark wrote, "That oil existed in Oklahoma in major deposits was undeniable. The giant discoveries in just the past decade had proven many petrologists wrong, but these so-called experts weren't good oilmen he knew, often remarking that a good oilman had a nose for oil."

E.W. knew that if he was right that oil lay beneath his feet, finding it would be easy. All it was going to take was a little luck and some money. Clark said, "Money was no problem. E.W. didn't have any, but he would get it. Luck was no problem either. He knew he had plenty of luck.

E.W. wondered if the oil strikes in the Bartlesville, Glenn Pool, and Red Fork fields could indicate the presence of an oil reservoir that possibly stretched for dozens, maybe even hundreds of miles. Was it possible that the oil bearing formations that lay to the east of the Osage could also extend to the west? The possibility, though a reach, did cross his mind."

On his visit to the 101 Ranch a few days later, E.W. walked for miles, studying the outcroppings of the rocks and inspecting formations. He was convinced oil lay beneath the ranch and he told George Miller he would drill a well if he could lease the ranch property. The potential for oil on the 101 Ranch caused E.W. to stay in Oklahoma—and he quickly forgot about going on to California.

BELOW: E.W. Marland with key men in his early oil and gas operations in Oklahoma. Left to right, Press Lowrance, Marland, W.H. "Bill" McFadden, and George Miller of the 101 Ranch.

Getting leases on land adjacent to the 101 Ranch was not easy. Dickering with landowners such as Peter-Knows-the-Country and Lean-Bear's-Ear, was difficult. E.W. said, "But after a lot of palaver, smoking, and squatting, we got the lands leased up and were ready to drill."

In February, 1909, E.W. staked out the first location for a test well. He used his letter of credit to buy equipment at the nearest Oil Well Supply Company location in Tulsa. The drilling equipment was shipped by rail to Bliss, the nearest spur to the well site. E.W. used ox teams to haul rig timbers, boilers, casing, and tools to the drilling location. Eventually, the derrick was up and drilling began on the spot where E.W.'s geological know-how had led him.

Everything that E.W. owned was involved in the drilling. He later remembered, "Every dollar I had in the world; every bit of credit I could muster; every hope I had was in that hole in the ground. It had to strike oil. If it didn't, it meant that I had to go to work for somebody else. It meant my entire future. I was either to be an employer or an employee from that time. If I had made a mistake of a few hundred feet I was through."

Unfortunately, the first test well drilled near ranch buildings on the 101 Ranch came up dry and was abandoned. E.W. scraped together a few dollars and kept going. The next seven wells produced gas, but they inspired little interest in E.W.'s dream. Gas had been found in Kay County before, but skeptics doubted there was any oil west of Osage County.

E.W. needed an investor to provide money for more drilling. He and George Miller visited W.H. McFadden, a sickly retired Carnegie Steel executive, who had moved to Hot Springs, Arkansas, to regain his health. McFadden, who believed he had been sent away from his home in Pittsburgh to die at Hot Springs, liked the idea of looking for oil in Kay County. It gave him optimism and hope. In early 1910, he agreed to fund the drilling of another well.

E.W. looked for a new site. At a place where Ponca Indians had placed their dead on wicker platforms above the ground, E.W. found what he believed was not only a topographic, but a structural high. The sacred ground, which lay within the Ponca reservation, was on an

ABOVE: Saturday afternoon was a busy time in Ponca City during E.W. Marland's first years in the town. Note the mixture of wagons, carriages, and horseless carriages. *Courtesy Ponca City News.*

allotment of Ponca Indian, Willie-Crys-for-War. The ideal spot where E.W. believed there was oil was where the land sloped toward "Bodark" Creek, called Bois d'Arc by the French, a tributary of the Salt Fork of the Arkansas River.

Working with White Eagle, chief of the Ponca, E.W. was able to secure a lease on the sacred land. Acquiring the lease would not have been possible, however, without the help of George Miller who had considerable influence with the Native Americans whose tribal lands he had leased and which comprised the bulk of the 101 Ranch.

Without sufficient funds to hire all his work done by others, E.W. personally drove the oxen from the railroad with loads of derrick timbers and equipment necessary to drill the new well. When drilling began, E.W. slept onsite and took his meals there. He bought cheap chuck roast, third-grade potatoes, and cheap onions to make mulligan stew in a tin pail over a cook fire. Without funds, he convinced Annie Rhoades, the owner of the Arcade Hotel, to extend him credit while he and Virginia were living there.

Though his first eight wells, some of which had shows of gas, were dry holes, E.W. remained optimistic. He strongly believed in his geological theories, and that luck would change. Later he would say, "There is nothing more interesting and exciting than standing with your back to a boiler on a cold winter day, examining the sand

RIGHT: Standing Bear, left, and White Eagle, chief of the Ponca tribe, pose for photographers after E.W. Marland hit oil on land he leased from the Poncas. *Courtesy Oklahoma Historical Society.*

to see whether you are a millionaire or a pauper." He exclaimed, "Talk about horse-racing as being the sport of kings! Then wild-catting must be the sport of emperors! When you get your fingers into the sand, you know whether you've got an empire or whether you haven't."

To carry on the operations, he organized the 101 Ranch Oil Company. First shareholders included W.H. McFadden, J.C. McCaskey, Franklin Kenney, and Lew Wentz.

E.W.'s wooden derrick on the flank of the hill dominated the landscape. It was one of the highest points for miles around and the clink-clank of the drilling operation disturbed the Ponca Indians living nearby. E.W. was vigilant over his project. During the last cold spell before spring, his rain-soaked clothing froze to his body and crackled as he bent over his mulligan stew.

E.W. was not at the well when oil was discovered. He was helping his crew lay a pipe line across the Salt Fork in July, 1911, when the driller hit 1,500 feet at which depth oil began bubbling out of the open hole. One of the crew ran to the White House to tell George Miller that oil was "showing in the well." Miller and Lew Wentz jumped into a buggy and raced to tell E.W. the news.

When the three men arrived at the location, the drilling crew had already pulled the tools out of the hole and a geyser of oil was spraying over the crown block. By this time, several Poncas had gathered, looking on in fear and astonishment. "Well, we found it!" E.W. smiled, "We finally hit oil." For years thereafter, people in Ponca City would call the Willie Crys for War "the famous ninth well" because the previous eight wells drilled by E.W. had been considered dry holes, though two of them had produced some gas.

E.W. did not need to make the startling announcement that oil had been hit because the air smelled of sulphur and the blackish spray was carried by the breeze to everything around the well. E.W.'s hands trembled. The workers bathed in the black liquid that covered their faces and clothing, slapped people on the back, and congratulated each other over and over.

Not everyone was excited. White Eagle told E.W. that he was making "bad medicine" for himself, the Ponca Tribe and the 101 Ranch, and E.W. If the chief, who died there years later, had lived long enough, he would have seen his "predictions" come true. Also less than enchanted by E.W.'s first gusher was another Ponca, Running-After-Arrow, who grunted, "No good, no good. Beautiful country all die now. Cattle die. Ponies die. Trees and grass die. No good, no good. Beautiful country soon all-gone."

But to E.W. the roar of the gas was worth years of study and failure. His faith in his own interpretation and utilization of geological evidence was vindicated. His discovery opened a new empire for oil production. The Ponca Field was born and new day had dawned for a vast region of north central Oklahoma.

It was an eventful beginning of using scientific methods for finding new oil supplies. The idea of just drilling a well and hoping to hit oil by luck would quickly give way to technology. E.W. had single handedly changed the way new oil reserves would be found forever.

BELOW: One of E.W. Marland's early investors in oil and gas ventures was Lew Wentz, born in Iowa, one of seven children of a blacksmith. Known as America's richest bachelor, Wentz teamed with Marland to develop oil fields around Ponca City. Wentz was known as "Daddy Long Legs" because he made certain every child in Ponca City had a coat and a pair of shoes. He lived in the Arcade Hotel for 38 years. He died in 1949, leaving his fortune to a trust that has educated thousands of university students with "Lew Wentz Scholarships." *Courtesy Oklahoma Historical Society.*

Oil Baron

SOME PEOPLE in the oil industry saw E.W. as an innovative leader, while others considered him a maverick. E.W. knew his discovery of oil was the beginning of a great new oil field in the middle of the North American continent. He also knew that, to be of value, oil had to be transported. He knew about the importance of transporting oil and gas. Back east, he had seen Standard Oil Company discourage and defeat competitors by owning means to transport crude.

Within three years, E.W. opened two other fields in Kay County. Other production soon began in fields at Tonkawa, Three Sands, Garber, Braman, and Billings. He was slightly disappointed when expected oil wells came in as gas wells. However, he built pipelines to supply the towns of Newkirk, Tonkawa, and Ponca with gas. One of the greatest gas wells came in near Newkirk. By 1913, the land around Blackwell was one of the world's great gas fields. E.W. built a pipe line to the Chilocco Indian School and into southern Kansas. The 101 Ranch Oil Company was really a gas company.

The first office building for the 101 Ranch Oil Company in Ponca was a one-story frame building. As news of his discovery spread, it was apparent that E.W. had a jump on other would-be developers of the Ponca field and other fields in Kay County. He formed his second company, Kay County Gas Company, to sell gas from wells in the vast sections of land he had leased. The new gas company took over 28 wells in the Blackwell area alone.

E.W. had proved to geologists that by drilling down through the eastern edges of the Permian Red Beds, a driller could reach the producing sands of the Pennsylvanian strata. E.W. knew that a huge area of land within driving distance of Ponca City would surely be developed over the next few years. He took steps to be at the forefront of that development.

In 1912, E.W. approached members of the School Land Commission to explore for oil on property set aside by the Oklahoma constitution for public schools in each township. Members of the School Land Commission, including the state superintendent of public instruction, were hungry for revenue and saw great potential in leasing their lands to E.W.

By the summer of 1912, E.W. had leased more than 130,000 acres of school lands. He paid only a $50 bonus to lease an entire section in Kay County, and little more for leases in Kay, Pawnee, and Kiowa counties.

E.W.'s deal with Oklahoma Governor Lee Cruce and the School Land Commission was that he would drill wells in the Blackwell field to prevent other operators from removing oil and gas from beneath school lands. The state would receive a one-eighth royalty on any production from the wells.

Some criticized E.W. for taking advantage of the school children of the state by paying such a paltry sum for the school land leases. However, he survived any political storm after a legislative investigating committee found that E.W. had done nothing wrong, although legislators concluded that the School Land Commission's agreement with E.W. was "imprudent."

Lydie Roberts, left, and her brother, George, outside a tent during a camping trip c. 1907. Lydie was seven and George was ten years old.

Even though E.W. returned to Pittsburgh in 1912 for a visit, he was deeply entrenched in Oklahoma. He and Mary Virginia liked Ponca City and its people, but there was a deeper reason for him wanting to stay in Oklahoma. He had heard of oil men coming into an area, making their millions, then heading south with the profits. He wanted to create a great company, to compete with Standard Oil, but he insisted on remaining in Ponca City to personally direct his company's operations, to create a spirit of fraternity among his workers.

E.W. was busy with his dream. He often had 20 to 30 wells being drilled simultaneously. A normal day would begin at dawn at Ponca City where he rode a buckboard with a team of horses 15 miles to Newkirk, looked over the operations, and spent the night in a work shack. The next day, he drove another 15 miles to Blackwell, then on to Tonkawa, and back to Ponca City. Each week, he made the 75-mile trip without fail. Often he went a week without taking off his boots. Most of his meals were out of a tin bucket. It would be years before he could say that he had as many meals off a dinner table as out of a dinner pail.

E.W. was proud of his Ponca discovery. In *My Experience With a Money Trust,* he wrote, "In a few years…I made millions of dollars, every dollar of which was taken from the ground, and the world was richer by reason of my finding and producing its natural resources. Not one dollar of my wealth was made by stock market gambling. Nobody lost what I had gained."

With E.W. gone most of the time, Mary Virginia longed for company. She had made good friends with other women in Ponca City, but she and E.W. had not been able to conceive children. In 1912, after nine years of marriage and no children, she invited the two oldest children of her older sister, Margaret Collins Roberts, to spend some time in Ponca City at their home in the Arcade Hotel.

The invitation to send her children to Oklahoma for a visit was welcomed by Margaret who felt sorry for her younger sister who had not been able to begin a family. Margaret and her husband, George Frederick Roberts, had four children. George, the only son of George W. Roberts, a Philadelphia dentist, was forced to earn a living as a wholesale produce dealer. His father had died when he was four years old and George F. barely made a living for his family in the early years living in Flourtown, a suburb of Philadelphia.

George Jr., the oldest of the four Roberts children, was born in Philadelphia on November 19, 1897. His oldest sister was Lydie Miller Roberts, born in Philadelphia on April 7, 1900. A second son was Ernest Marland Roberts, born April 27, 1904. The fourth child was Mary Virginia, named for Mary Virginia Marland, born July 3, 1909.

George and Margaret were excited about George Jr. and Lydie, ages 14 and 12, spending some time with E.W. and Mary Virginia in Oklahoma. The well-to-do Marlands could certainly provide for the children better than their father. But, George and Margaret rebuffed

Mary Virginia's plea that George Jr. and Lydie live with them for three or four years. Instead, they agreed that the children could move to Oklahoma for one year.

The children were dressed in their finest clothes when Mary Virginia arrived to take them back to Oklahoma. Margaret was devastated that her children would be gone for awhile, but she also knew that feeding four people, rather than six, would decrease the pressure on her husband who worked from daylight to dark to make his produce business successful.

The children were sad to leave their parents and their younger siblings, but they also looked forward to the adventure of visiting another part of America. They knew their lifestyle would be comfortable—after all, they would in the future travel around the country in E.W.'s private rail car, "The Ponca City."

After the long train ride to Oklahoma, the children settled in with Mary Virginia and E.W. in a suite at the Arcade Hotel. They were given things beyond their expectation, took long vacations in Europe, and hosted lavish parties for their friends. Before Lydie had arrived in Oklahoma, Mary Virginia had used Ruth McDowell, who was the same age and size as Lydie, as a model for clothing. Mary Virginia would have Ruth, who later married Robert E. Clark, come to the Marland suite at the Arcade Hotel to be measured. Ruth was one of Lydie's first playmates. As they became teenagers, Lydie was shy, especially with boys.

The hotel suite became too small for the Marlands so they moved into a private home at 318 North Sixth Street in Ponca City. The home had four bedrooms and was nearly new. There was also a basement to provide more room for the family that had doubled in size with the arrival of George Jr. and Lydie. The Marlands would make the frame house on Sixth Street their home for nearly four years.

E.W. and Mary Virginia adopted George Jr. and Lydie in 1916. It is a mystery under what circumstances their parents would allow the formal adoption and change of their last name, although legend has it that E.W. paid George Roberts $50,000 in exchange for George and his wife's surrender of their parental rights and their approval of the adoption of their two oldest children. Another factor may have been the financial stress that was created when the three daughters of George's sister came to live with the family after her death in 1913. Still another factor might have been the fact that Margaret had lost three children in the previous 15 years to sickness and disease.

E.W. intended for George and Lydie to receive the finest education possible. Lydie, a beautiful young girl, who preferred that her friends call her Lyde, and spell her name accordingly, was given an outstanding education. She did not attend public schools but had a private tutor in Ponca City and was then sent to the finest finishing schools. She attended a girls' school, Monticello College, in Monticello, Illinois, Mrs. Spence's School for Girls in New York, and Miss Merrill's School in Mamaroneck, New York. Later, she graduated from a finishing

E.W. Marland built a 22-room mansion on Grand Avenue in 1916. The house had an indoor swimming pool.

school called Oaksmere at Mamaroneck on Long Island, New York.

Records at Monticello show Lydie enrolled in classes in English, French, history, physical education, Bible, spelling, piano, and ukulele in the 14 months she was there in 1917 and 1918.

George attended St. Mary's High School in Ponca City and enrolled in college at Yale University in New Haven, Connecticut. To be closer to the children, E.W. and Mary Virginia spent long periods of time at their suite at the Plaza Hotel in New York City. On short school breaks, George and Lydie were taken for visits to their parents and younger brother and sister in Flourtown. In 1920, the Roberts purchased their own home, a two-story house in Flourtown.

When she was not in school, Lydie returned to Ponca City to host parties for her friends at the Marland's first mansion completed in 1916 on Grand Avenue at Tenth Street. Living in the roomy house on Sixth Street had been fine, but moving into the 22-room mansion was divine. The big white stucco house had an indoor swimming pool and beautifully landscaped grounds. Its formal, terraced gardens contained the most beautiful collection of flowers, shrubs, and foliage west of the Mississippi River.

E.W. personally oversaw the development of his gardens by Henry Hatashita, a master gardener from Japan. E.W. purchased 80 acres at first, then added to it to provide space for his gardens and a nine-hole golf course. The lands that were now his gardens had once been a maize

LEFT: An aerial view of the Grand Avenue mansion, at left of the photograph, and the artistically landscaped grounds that were hailed as the most beautiful collection of flowers, shrubs, and foliage west of the Mississippi River.

RIGHT: Looking east from the veranda of the Marland home on East Grand Avenue. At the end of the walkway is a huge greenhouse that provided plants for the spacious gardens. The Marland home is now called Marland's Grand Home.

Mary Virginia Marland, portrayed by Nancy Mott, reading in the library of the home on East Grand Avenue. *Courtesy M.A. Crank.*

Through the magic of photography, E.W. and Mary Virginia Marland walk down the magnificent stairs at the Marland Grand Home. The Marlands were portrayed by Mike and Nancy Mott. *Courtesy M.A. Crank.*

and corn field. The tract upon which the golf course was located was a treeless field used in part as a city dump.

Three miles of Amur River privet hedge were planted around the golf course. From the Arkansas River bottoms came 400 trees. Concrete walks were added, along with hundreds of shrubs from all over the United States. E.W. wanted everyone in town to enjoy the nine-hole course so no green fee was charged and golf clubs were provided free to anyone who wanted to play on the course run by his golf professional, Sandy McDonald. It took 30 men to keep the golf course and gardens in perfect condition.

E.W. was so enamored with his plans to make the grounds of his new home luxurious, he sent his head gardener, Henry Hatashita, on a year-long, round-the-world trip in 1923 to gather information about flowers and plants. Hatashita first went to England, then to France and on to Japan. While in Japan, the country was hit with a devastating earthquake that killed more than 100,000 people. E.W. did not hear from Hatashita for two months, fearing they had been lost in the earthquake. Fortunately, Hatashita and his wife were spared and returned to their work in Ponca City.

As family life developed for E.W., Mary Virginia, and their two adopted children, E.W.'s oil interests blossomed. The Marland operation was huge. In addition to the refinery, tank farms, a six-story office building, and 1,000 houses had been built. In 1915, E.W. organized the Marland Oil Company of Oklahoma. New companies were organized to control various phases of the production business.

In 1916, the Marland refinery was built in Ponca City, tripling the population of the town. Two years later, it was capable of processing 30,000 barrels of crude oil a day. With the ability to produce gasoline, E.W. went into the retail business. The sign of the Marland red triangle became familiar across America.

E.W. had selected this logo from several designed by his close friend Gene Waldo who was in the import-export business in New York City and was also a gifted artist. E.W. already admired the red triangle concept because of

RIGHT: An artist's conception of a tank car owned by Marland Refining Company. *Courtesy Conoco.*

E.W. Marland surrounded by some of the children who lived at the American Legion children's home funded by Marland in Ponca City.

his work with the Young Mens' Christian Association (YMCA) during World War I. He sought and received permission from the YMCA to use a similar logo for his company.

E.W. wanted each of his automobile filling stations to be attractive to customers. Some of the stations built were in the shape of a triangle, synonymous with the Marland Oil logo. Each station also was surrounded by flowers and shrubs. By 1927, there were 550 Marland Oil stations in 11 states.

From 1915 to 1922, E.W. created a number of wholly owned subsidiaries, most with limited stockholders. Many of the stockholders in the diversified companies were the same original investors in the 101 Ranch Oil Company. Most of the companies such as the Tom James

OIL BARON

Within 20 miles of the Marland Oil Company refinery in Ponca City were oil fields that were expected to supply the refinery with crude oil for years. *Courtesy Ponca City News.*

Oil Company, Kenney-Cleary Oil Company, Frankoma Oil Company, John Alcorn Oil Company, People's Fuel Supply Company, Marland Production Company, Marland Refining Company, Comar Oil Company, Reagan County Purchasing Company, Hudson's Bay Marland Oil Company, and Marland Oil Company of Mexico were profitable, but cumbersome. Many of them had been formed to sidestep federal government regulations that one company could not secure more than 4,800 acres of oil leases in the Osage Nation.

Shareholders had done well investing in E.W.'s production programs. J.J. McGraw and George Miller turned $1,250 investments into $125,000 when sold to Josh Cosden.

In 1920, E.W. followed the advice of his attorneys and organized Marland Oil Company as a holding company for a score of subsidiary companies. At age 46, E.W. was ambitious to build a completely integrated oil company that would take its place at the pinnacle of America's petroleum industry. He told his friends that he had all the money he ever wanted. His personal fortune was estimated at more than $100 million. Over a ten-year period, he paid income taxes of more than $3.6 million—an average of $1,000 a day.

Marland Oil Company was incorporated in Delaware. It was born big and rapidly grew larger. It was a complete company—producing raw crude, refining it into motor fuel and lubricating oil, and transporting in its own tank cars or ocean tankers to its own service stations and bulk plants, or to the stations of dealers or jobbers.

ABOVE: The first trainload of gasoline leaves the Marland Refinery.

OIL BARON 45

E.W. was kind to the men who had grown up with him in the success of his ventures. He became the employer of about one-third of the adult working population of Ponca City. He was never, however, an arm-around-the-shoulder type of guy. And while his closest friends always called him E.W., the rank and file continued to address him as Mr. Marland. Still, he was a compassionate, altruistic man who believed that his people should make not only a living wage, but a saving wage.

He made it easy for employees to buy housing by making available low-interest loans from his bank. He lavishly rewarded his workers who made new discoveries. He gave huge blocks of stocks to his officers. Employee benefits were at least a quarter century ahead of their time. Marland Oil offered free medical and dental care.

The Marland Industrial Institute, a school for employees, gave everyone a chance for improvement. It was a concept far ahead of its time. The school consisted of a series of buildings located on a bluff northeast of Ponca City, created in Spanish colonial style with stucco finish. The buildings housed a cafeteria, swimming pool, tennis courts, dorm rooms, classrooms, a lecture hall, library, kitchen, and other recreational facilities.

Both Marland Oil department heads and guest instructors taught Marland employees courses in accounting, geology, petroleum engineering, taxation, and refining. Years later, the institute was closed and sat vacant until the Ponca Military Academy occupied the premises beginning in about 1940.

ABOVE: E.W. Marland built a headquarters office building adjacent to his refinery southwest of Ponca City. Later, the building was expanded by Conoco. On the original building's top floor is Marland's restored office.

The first home of Marland Refining Company was in downtown Ponca City on South First Street.

ABOVE: The renovated Conoco board room as it appears today, complete with a portrait of E.W. Marland over the fireplace. The paneling is American walnut. The table, crafted especially for Marland, came from an old ship he had purchased. *Courtesy Robert Burke.*

ABOVE: When Conoco renovated its headquarters building, the room which had been E.W. Marland's office was restored to its original size by removing partitions which had separated it into four rooms. The old map with the Marland red triangle was found and redisplayed over the fireplace which is black Italian marble. *Courtesy Robert Burke.*

LEFT: A Marland Oil Company worker prepares accounting information for investors.

RIGHT: The familiar red and white logo of Marland Oil Company.

ABOVE: Marland Oil Company trucks line up outside the refining company warehouse.

LEFT: The English lime wood carvings above the fireplace in the Conoco board room portray the then-used implements of the oil industry and flowers of the Southwest. *Courtesy Robert Burke.*

E.W. also generously gave to almost every public cause in Ponca City, from construction of parks and an airfield to giving land to the Sisters of St. Joseph to build a hospital. He also raised funds and gave land to start the Oklahoma American Legion Home School, for dependents of World War I veterans.

Once when asked why he gave so much money for the betterment of Ponca City, E.W. said, "I spent money like water on my people and on my town. They flourished and the town blossomed like a rose. The people were happy and contented. And they made money for me at a great rate. Some of my lieutenants may have been spoiled by good fortune, but not many. The town was too small and everyone knew everyone else too well to permit anyone becoming high hat. Mutual respect and friendship between the offices and the men made the hardest kind of work a joy. The atmosphere of opportunity and reward helped solve many a tough technical problem."

ABOVE: Marland Refining Company trucks deliver gasoline to a Marland Oil Company filling station.

LEFT: At a cost of $65,000, Marland Oil built this automobile filling station on North Classen Boulevard in Oklahoma City in 1923. On the station's first day in business, a world record 20,000 gallons of gasoline was sold from 6:00 a.m. to 10:00 p.m.

One possible motivation for E.W.'s sharing with his employees and townspeople was that he subconsciously remembered his narrow escape from the ranks of the employed.

Marland Oil's geological staff managed to keep ahead of its competition for years. Marland Oil carefully guarded its trade secrets from the scouting department of other companies. E.W. hired some of the world's most famous geologists to work in his research department.

E.W. introduced the use of the core drill a year ahead of the rest of the industry. F. Park "Spot" Geyer, a football star whose nickname came from his ability to throw a pass to an exact spot, headed the Marland Oil geological department that began using the German-developed seismograph two years before other oil companies.

E.W. expanded his horizons and was granted a concession on thousands of square miles of potential oil property in Mexico in 1919. In the states of Sinaloa and Sonora he had exploration rights on nine million acres, the largest concession ever granted to a foreigner by the Mexican government.

The roaring twenties were great for E.W. and Marland Oil Company. The Burbank field was discovered in 1920 and the Tonkawa field was opened the following year. Each of those two major pools produced more than 100,000 barrels a day.

In the summer of 1921, E.W. visited Sir Henri Deterding in London and organized the Comar Oil Company, jointly owned by Marland Oil and the Royal Dutch Shell Company. Marland only invested $1 million in the venture, but made more than $25 million from exploration and development in Mexico and South America during the next five years.

A by-product of E.W.'s involvement with Royal Dutch Shell was his hiring of Dr. W.A.J.M. van Waterschoot van der Gracht, a native of Holland, as director of Marland's scientific research department. Van der Gracht was considered one of the world's leading geologists.

By 1923, E.W. surrounded himself with two dozen men who played key roles in managing the affairs of the growing Marland Oil Company. McFadden was executive vice president, W.G. Lackey, was vice president of finance, J.S. Alcorn was vice president in charge of administration, and Franklin Kenney headed up the California office. Samuel C. Collins, E.W.'s brother-in-law, was in charge of marketing. Charley C. Brown ran the production and pipeline department. John Hale was E.W.'s confidante and personal assistant.
Chester

LOWER LEFT: E.W. Marland's private rail car, the "Ponca City," was built in 1920 originally for the Mexican government, to be the private luxury car of President Francisco Madero. The car even had bullet-proof windows. However, the Madero government was overthrown by Pancho Villa and Marland bought the rail car from the manufacturer. The interior of the rail car was something to behold, maintained by Marland employees to a high standard of luxury.

Westfall was manager of Mexican and Central American operations.

Earl Oliver was manager of the economics department and had earlier headed up the company office in Mexico City. George Shallenberger, the former president of Kay County Gas Company, was in charge of natural gas activities. All of these men were well educated and extremely talented. For example, Seward Sheldon was one of three Phi Beta Kappas hired by E.W. from the University of Oklahoma from 1913 to 1915. The other two were geologists Glen Clark and Fritz Aurin. Seward succeeded Bill Lackey as company treasurer in 1926.

Walter Miller was in charge of refining, John K. Cleary headed the land department. George Marland, E.W.'s adopted son, was a director of the company and worked in the refining end of the business.

E.W. and his company were flying high. His worldwide notoriety in the petroleum industry allowed him to borrow huge sums of money at banks all over the country to finance new construction of pipelines and tank farms for storage of the expanding production of his vast empire. At one point in the 1920s, E.W. controlled 10 percent of the world's known oil reserves.

E.W. Marland hosted lavish picnics for his employees and friends at the Bar L pasture in the bend of the Arkansas River. Marland is wearing a bow tie and vest, sitting at the center of the photograph. For picnics, Marland workers built a wooden dancing floor, pitched tents for guests, and dug fire pits for a huge kitchen tent.

Princess Lydie

THERE IS NO DOUBT that Lydie Marland became the princess of the Marland empire in the 1920s. While Mary Virginia was content with a quiet life and long visits with her friends from church, Lydie concentrated on learning all she could about art, music, and especially, dance. She also enjoyed going on fox hunts with E.W. or watching polo matches. Lydie often met E.W. at the train station when he returned from business trips.

Mary Virginia was not in the best of health and shied away from many parties and public functions. John Cleary remembered, "She did not share her husband's love of public acclaim, hence their receptions and dinner parties were few and far between. Weekly get-togethers of the most informal character usually took place in the big room downstairs."

Mary Virginia's chronic illness, probably cancer, took her to Kansas City, Missouri, for treatment with Dr. Abraham Sophian. Not knowing how long Mary Virginia would be under Sophian's care, E.W. bought a 24-room brick Georgian colonial home on Sunset Drive in a prestigious neighborhood in Kansas City. He paid $82,500 for the home from its owner, Lyman Reed.

In 1917-1918, Lydie came to visit Mary Virginia from Monticello College in Godfrey, Illinois, as did E.W. from Ponca City. A frequent visitor in the home on Sunset Drive was Ruth McDowell who was attending Spaulding Business College in Kansas City at the same time. She, Mary Virginia, and Lydie shopped together and attended stage shows and concerts. When Lydie was in town, Ruth was invited to spend the weekend.

Stories have always circulated in Kansas City that E.W. was so thankful that Dr. Sophian had cured his wife, he gave the home to the doctor. However, property records show E.W. never personally owned the home, but city directories record him living there in the early 1920s.

When Mary Virginia returned home to Ponca City, her illness grew progressively worse. However, when she was well enough, she hosted parties and traveled with E.W. to Cuba, the Bahamas, the Caribbean, and up the Ohio River

to the Kentucky Derby, aboard their yacht, *Whitemarsh*. Lydie, when home from college or her travels, often served as hostess at the Marland home on Grand Avenue, but only when Mary Virginia was absent.

Lydie and her brother George were textbook children, seldom giving E.W. and Mary Virginia major problems. Following service in World War I, George attended the University of Oklahoma for one year, then moved to Yale University where he graduated. He was nice looking, gregarious, with an easy manner that enabled him to make friends easily. He spent much of this early 1920s living the good life in Ponca City, once co-writing a play, all the while working for his father's oil company.

On the other hand, Lydie was somewhat demure, even withdrawn, except with her closest friends, yet she was comely, five feet four inches, 115 pounds, with an attractive figure. Her unbobbed brown hair framed a pretty face in which were set big, brown, but doleful eyes.

Lydie never dated anyone seriously, at least not for long. William "Bill" Frothingham was

LEFT: Lydie Roberts Marland on the veranda of the Marland home on Grand Avenue. *Courtesy Robert Clark, Jr.*

ABOVE: Lydie entertained at lavish parties for her friends. Left to right, Gwen Nelson, Bill Frothingham, a guest from Boston, Massachusetts, Lydie, and Ruth McDowell. Courtesy Robert Clark, Jr.

one of her suitors. From Boston, and a Harvard graduate, he was a land man in E.W.'s Wichita, Kansas, office. They dated on occasion but he was more interested in Lydie than she was in him.

Lydie's Eastern education gave her a great appreciation for the arts, and for parties. Her friends believed she was truly at ease at parties with friends on the back veranda of the home on Grand Avenue. She loved to dance and pose for a friend's camera, although if a newspaper reporter happened to be on the grounds, she was likely to vanish. She was fiercely private.

ABOVE: Lydie Roberts Marland at a party at Gwen Moore's house in 1914. Left to right, back row, Ruth McDowell, Rose Soldani, Marie Hall, Jessie Scott, and Annie Lee Broaddus. Sitting, left to right, Marjorie Panton, Lydie, and Gwen Moore. *Courtesy Robert Clark, Jr.*

RIGHT: Lydie Marland and friend, Don Walker, in 1919. *Courtesy Robert Clark, Jr.*

PRINCESS LYDIE

LEFT: The hand-drawn cover to a play written by George Marland and Harold Osborn and performed by George, Lydie, and their Ponca City friends. *Courtesy Robert Clark, Jr.*

BELOW: George Roberts Marland, right, and friend, Harold Boyson, pose for a photograph for "funny books," collections of photographs and stories exchanged by friends in Ponca City. *Courtesy Robert Clark, Jr.*

LEFT: Lydie became princess of the Marland empire as Mary Virginia Marland's health failed.

BELOW: A Shakespearian party at Edward Donahoe's house in July, 1922. Left to right, standing, George Marland as Hamlet, Edward Donahoe as Othello, Tot Boggess as King Lear, and Bill Frothingham as Mark Anthony. Seated, left to right, Jane Richie as Roasamund, Dorothy Omart as Lady McBeth, Ruth McDowell as Portia, Rebecca Sarchet as Ophelia, Peg Boggess as Cleop, and Lydie as Juliet. Reclining on the floor is Dee Donahoe as Caesar. *Courtesy Robert Clark, Jr.*

Lydie was supportive of E.W.'s great love for Ponca City and his willingness to give to almost every cause. He built playgrounds and baseball diamonds and gave unselfishly to the Boy Scouts, Girl Scouts, YMCA, medical research foundations, and churches, regardless of denomination.

The *Ponca City News* recognized E.W.'s importance, "Ponca City has been very fortunate in the possession of Ernest W. Marland as a citizen, a possession that has been the envy of many other cities not only in Oklahoma but elsewhere…for he is a national figure, both in the oil industry and as the man who does things for his hometown, being very liberal and willing at all times to assist in whatever program the city may have."

In 1924, E.W. hired Tulsa architect John Duncan "Jack" Forsyth to design a new home on land E.W. had been acquiring for several years immediately northeast of Ponca City. After World War I, E.W. spotted a half-section of land containing a large limestone quarry that was then leased by the Santa Fe Railroad. He often walked the tract and envisioned the creation of a sanctuary for native birds and animals. He remarked to friends that the quarry's excavation would make a great swimming pool and bed of a lake.

In 1921, after the Santa Fe abandoned the quarry, E.W. bought the half section of land and began purchasing adjacent properties. Eventually, the Marland Estate holdings would exceed 2,000 acres. Around the original half section, E.W. erected a six-foot cyclone fence that stretched on its western perimeter along 14th Street from Highland to Hartford avenues. Within a short time, the mile-long fence was covered in spring and summer with red and white roses.

To his closest friends, E.W. described plans to build a lake with eight islands, rock gardens, riding stables, bridle paths, and fish ponds. He wanted to plant grain fields to entice turkey, pheasant, geese, duck, and quail to live on the premises. The acreage was to be a game refuge, with no hunting allowed. He also envisioned his other properties and the surrounding country as a locale to hold group rides and fox hunts.

At first, E.W.'s idea was to build just a summer house on the 300-acre tract which he called the "game refuge." He wanted the summer house to have luxurious but relaxing accommodations with several guest rooms, a place where his friends, out of town visitors, and business associates could unwind with him. But as plans for the summer house evolved into a more pretentious home, Forsyth became increasingly interested, packing up a portfolio of ideas and traveling to Estes Park, Colorado, where E.W. was on vacation. At the end of a three-day meeting, E.W. hired Forsyth.

Prior to Forsyth's involvement, the concept of the smaller, more intimate summer cottage had grown into a Spanish-style hacienda, and later into a Roman villa with red-tiled roofs, wrought iron grillwork, and walled privacy. After listening to Forsyth's proposal, E.W. became excited by his ideas. His own vision of developing the property moved from building a cozy cottage for small cocktail parties, card games, and billiards, to an opulent, formal venue that could accommodate

E.W. Marland brought workmen from all over the world to build the Marland Mansion.

large gatherings. And, instead of one lake, five smaller lakes would be built to better sectionalize the refuge.

Construction on the palatial home and development of the grounds began in 1925. Forsyth hired a skilled group of artists, stone masons, architects, and sculptors of international reputation to create and embellish what would be called the "Palace on the Prairie."

As the foundation of the home was being prepared, dozens of workmen began building five lakes, two of which would flank the mansion on the north and south exposures. The final design

ABOVE In 1926, workers take a break alongside the pool of water that would become the Marland Mansion swimming pool.

RIGHT: In 1927, construction was nearing completion on the Marland Mansion.

for the house was for a pretentious Roman villa with formidable walls of native stone, topped with a roof of red tile, a porte cochere, terraces, and exterior stairways. Wrought-iron Mediterranean grillwork was imported to grace both the inside and outside of the home. To the extent Oklahoma soil and climate permitted, the lakes were intended to proximate the luxuriance of Italian lake district estates.

During the construction of the lakes, E.W. continued to insist that the aquatic environment be a harmonious habitat for waterfowl and other wildlife. Landscape craftsmen mapped out plans for gardens, fish ponds, walkways, and bridle paths, while architects mulled over ideas for a guest house, boat house, servant's quarters, garages, and riding stables.

Mary Virginia, who was growing more sickly and was being treated with several different kinds of drugs, wanted large rose and vegetable gardens. Her idea was to have fresh flowers daily for the house and Oklahoma-grown vegetables such as okra, onions, snap beans, and tomatoes for the dinner table.

The two lakes flanking the mansion were to be connected by a 100-foot canal banked in limestone riprap, not only to provide an aesthetic ambience to the grounds, but to supply the south lake with a continual source of water.

In the south lake, there were five islands planted with flowers, trees, and shrubs. The north lake, created to mirror an Old World façade, and later to be called Whitemarsh, the same name as E.W.'s yacht, was to be ringed with trees and scarp wall. On the north lake, plans called for the construction of a Venice-styled boathouse. Two underground tunnels would run under landscaped grounds from both the mansion and artist's studio to the boathouse.

The west lake was farthest from the mansion and contained two islands called Turtle and Snake by the neighborhood children who frequented the premises and spent many an idle hour fishing, boating, swimming, and frog hunting. When the ice froze solid enough, children ice skated on the lake.

While Mary Virginia's illness kept her from actively participating in the planning and construction of the mansion, Lydie at times seemed even less interested in the project. She was busy traveling and entertaining friends she had made in social circles in the East and California, seldom visiting the mansion property.

After construction of the mansion was well underway, Mary Virginia died after a long illness on June 6, 1926. The official cause of death was pneumonia, although her friends said Mary

Dirt ruts approach the Marland Mansion as it neared completion.

Virginia died of cancer. At her funeral, there was a huge display of support from townspeople. It took two large automobiles to transport flowers to her final burial place at the cemetery.

Following Mary Virginia's death, Lydie increasingly assumed the role of hostess at the Grand Avenue Marland home. She had reached age 26, looking chic in designer clothing and planning social gatherings for E.W.'s friends.

Meanwhile, work continued on the mansion and grounds. Sparing no expense, E.W. gathered artisans from all over the world to work on his palace. One of the most notable artists

RIGHT: The Marland boathouse was a modern structure that was linked to the main house by a tunnel, and by a second tunnel to the artist studio.

CENTER: The elaborate gatehouse at the Marland Mansion was built on the shore of one of the estate's lakes.

FAR RIGHT: The garage and chauffeur's quarters that later became Lydie Marland's home in her final years.

The Marland Mansion in all its glory, surrounded by gardens and lakes.

was Vincent Margliotti, a world-renowned Italian mural artist. He and his helpers created masterpieces in the ornately painted ceilings in the mansion.

An example of the "no-expense spared" theme was the price tag for the ceiling in one room. E.W. paid $80,000 for sheets of 24 carat gold that were hammered leaf thin and applied with adhesive to the ceiling. Other ceilings were hand painted, with artists laying on scaffolding to paint above them, reminiscent of the Sistine Chapel.

The ceiling in the inner lounge was unique. One of Margliotti's assistants spent six weeks in Washington, D.C., studying Oklahoma history before painting a history of Kay County on the ceiling. The beams reflect the history from pre-Columbian Indians to the oil rigs of the 1920s. The ceiling is now considered to be an outstanding art treasure unmatched anywhere in the United States.

The palace was designed with many long, continuous walls so E.W.'s extensive art collection could be exhibited in gallery style. Silver light fixtures, crystal chandeliers, stained glass window scenes, curved marble staircases, and terrazzo tiled floors filled the house.

Angels of all types were prevalent in the Marland Mansion. Some were rich in detail, others were formed in stone and carved into wood furniture. A contrast to the angels were the many dragons added to the look of the mansion. Both inside and outside, dragons were added in stone and wrought-iron. The Swedish stone carver, Conrad Berglund, and Italian stone carver Pelligrini added the mythological creatures to corbels on the north terrace support of E.W.'s balcony. No one ever knew why dragons were so prominent in the design, although the architect and his family had spent time in China prior to beginning the mansion.

The final estimates of construction costs of the mansion and its accoutrements and outbuildings exceeded $5 million.

E.W. commissioned his favorite sculptor, Jo Davidson, to create from French limestone life-sized statues of Lydie, George, and himself. All three statues were placed prominently on the mansion grounds within gardens and hedgerows.

In 1927, E.W. proposed to erect a large statue in Ponca City to honor the brave women who had helped settle the western frontier, a statue dramatizing the pioneer woman in heroic pose. He asked 12 of the nation's most prominent sculptors to submit a model for which they would each be paid $10,000.

In a speech to the 12 sculptors and other invited guests at a dinner in New York City in February, 1927, E.W. pointed out that while hundreds of statues in the United States honored men, only a few paid tribute to women. He believed pioneer women had been overlooked by historians. He went on to say, "We, here, who have had a part in designing a monument to the pioneer woman of America, to be erected in the Cherokee Strip of Oklahoma, where she finished her last task of settling the land formerly occupied by Indians, and evolving civilization of the West, should be proud that we have had this opportunity to pay our tribute to the most heroic figure in all history."

The 12 miniature three-foot statues toured the country by train, traveling to a dozen different cities in six months. More than 750,000 people saw the statues and most voted for the model sculpted by Bryant Baker of New York, whose monument was of a confident woman and her young son. The 12 miniatures were later purchased by oil man Frank Phillips and are on display in the Woolaroc Museum near Bartlesville, Oklahoma.

Baker's model was selected and E.W. provided funds for the creation of the Pioneer Woman Statue to stand at Monument Circle, one block from the Marland Mansion. E.W. presented the 17-feet high and 12,000-pound statue to

A magnificent gazebo with a tile roof was an example of John Duncan Forsyth's genius in designing the grounds that surrounded the mansion.

LEFT: A statue of Lydie was placed in the venue north of the mansion. Years later, Lydie ordered the destruction of the statue.

BELOW: Children enjoy ducks swimming on one of the lakes on the Marland Estate grounds.

the State of Oklahoma and her people. Three years later when the statue was unveiled, more than 40,000 people gathered to hear dignitaries including Oklahoma humorist Will Rogers, who was the keynote speaker.

Although their closeness had long been noticed by many, E.W. and Lydie still shocked both friends and the public when they announced in January, 1928, that they were to be married. He was 54—she was 28. Friends were shocked because, as Bob Clark, said, "Riding horseback together was one thing—getting married was quite another."

One newspaper story said "Joint interests in polo, in development of the widely-known Marland gardens, in horseback riding, and other activities which the oil millionaire has sponsored" brought the two together.

Another report said, "Devotion between the couple was noticed in the loyalty with which she met the trains when Marland would return from his many trips away from Ponca City and in the pleasure they seemed to find in each other's company at parties and social events in recent months."

Four days after the engagement announcement, E.W. and Lydie took his private rail car back to Pennsylvania to have his adoption of her 12 years earlier annulled. As expected, the nation's press had a heyday with the news that the powerful oil baron, E.W. was to marry his adopted daughter.

After the annulment of the adoption, Lydie spent a few days in Atlantic City, New Jersey, while E.W. returned to Ponca City to take care of pressing business matters and to check on the mansion which was nearing completion.

The interior resembled a palace in Florence, Italy. When the mansion was formally opened

on June 2, 1928, E.W. hosted a daytime party for children and an evening gala for adults. The daytime event featured a sit-down luncheon, vaudeville acts with Shetland ponies, dogs, and monkeys, hayrides and games. Each child was given a silver loving cup with his or her name engraved on it. The evening party was a formal affair with a full dinner, cocktails, and dancing to the music of a big name orchestra.

In the year following Mary Virginia's death, E.W. and Lydie had been seen with increasing frequency at fox hunts, group rides, and polo matches. Although horse shows and rodeos had long been in vogue in Ponca City, polo commenced in earnest in 1923 when E.W. hired former English army major and prominent European polo player Donald L. Henderson as player-manager of the Ponca City Polo Association.

Henderson, who also was a MFH, master of fox hounds, brought a new and unique culture to Ponca City with the introduction of polo and fox hunting. Will Rogers and Tom Mix, among other notables, participated in polo matches in Ponca City in the 1920s.

E.W. was greatly responsible for the growth of polo in Ponca City, though all members of the local association bought their own horses and equipment, and paid their own veterinary bills. Some of the members, including Jack Cleary, Dillard Clark, and John Alcorn, built their own stables.

LEFT: A breezeway and gate on the mansion's west wall.

RIGHT: The winter room of the inner lounge.

A huge iron gate framed the completed Marland Mansion in 1928.

RIGHT: Ornate ceilings and arches were part of the design of the mansion.

LEFT: Sculptor Bryant Baker examines the completed Pioneer Woman Statute.

ABOVE: Every attention to detail was given to construction of the Marland Mansion. Note the ceiling above the foyer.

RIGHT: At the Pioneer Woman Statue dedication are, left to right, sculptor Bryant Baker, Mrs. George Hall, W.H. McFadden, and E.W. Marland. In the photograph at right is the hand of Lydie Marland. The original photograph that appeared in *The Daily Oklahoman* contained Lydie. However, when she had the photograph reproduced in the 1970s, she apparently intentionally deleted her image, characteristic of her feelings that she was unworthy of all the attention.

More than 40,000 people attended the dedication of the Pioneer Woman Statue. Humorist Will Rogers was the main attraction of a host of politicians and famous people on the program.

George Marland enthusiastically participated in the sport and later assumed managerial responsibilities of the association from Don Henderson after the Henderson family moved from Ponca City in 1930.

By 1928, as many as 30 riders out of the 62-member association participated in matches against polo teams that came to Ponca City from as far away as Chicago, Illinois, and Houston, Texas. Captains were elected each year for the city's four teams and included John Alcorn, Don Henderson, George Shallenberger, C.E. Northcutt, George Marland, and Foy Crawford.

Members of United States Army teams who played in Ponca City included Jacob Devers, Lucian Truscott, George Patton, Jonathan M. Wainwright, and George Gay, all who later became generals, commanding American forces during World War II.

In addition to the polo team, E.W. organized regular fox hunts and horse shows. Cavalry squadrons were formed for youngsters depending on age. Many of the town's children participated in drills and sham battles, as well as other equestrian events, all under E.W.'s watchful eye and enthusiastic support. George Marland and many others in town built large stables for their polo ponies, show horses, and jumpers.

On July 14, 1928, six weeks after the formal opening of the Marland Mansion, E.W. and Lydie returned to Philadelphia where they were married. Again the tabloids screamed nasty headlines. E.W. was hurt and Lydie was crushed. Some of the pain was eased by an extensive honeymoon across southern Canada and Hudson Bay and onto California. E.W. mixed business with pleasure by checking on his oil interests both in Canada and California.

After several weeks of honeymooning, E.W. and Lydie returned to Ponca City and quietly moved into their new home, "The Palace on the Prairie."

Hundreds of friends and Ponca City citizens flocked to the mansion in June, 1928, for the opening of the Marland Mansion.

ABOVE: The hand-drawn invitation to the opening party at the Marland Mansion on June 2, 1928. Note the invitation referred to the estate as "The Refuge," the name used by E.W. Marland to describe his multi-million dollar construction project.

LEFT: The Ponca City Blues won the 1927 polo tournament in Ponca City. Left to right, George Marland, Foy Crawford, George Shallenberger, and Curtis Allen.

E.W. Marland built personal stables to house horses he used in competition events, polo, and on fox hunts. The stable, of French architecture, was originally built to house work teams for the mansion construction. When polo became popular, wings formerly used to house equipment and a blacksmith shop were converted into box stalls.

ABOVE: Walter Miller, vice president of Marland Oil Company, was a regular referee for polo matches in Ponca City.

LEFT: A copy of the marriage license issued by Montgomery County, Pennsylvania, for E.W. and Lydie Roberts after the annulment of her adoption. E.W. and Lydie were married in Flourtown, Pennsylvania, by the rector of St. Thomas Church in Whitemarsh, Pennsylvania, on July 14, 1928.

The Takeover

AS VISITORS ENTERED the newly-completed Marland Estate, they were introduced to breathtaking sights. In springtime, a mass of blooming pink and red tulips and three miles of roses along fences and stone walls created an atmosphere not found anywhere else in the central part of the United States.

A crew of 85 gardeners meticulously kept the estate. Surrounding the mansion were lakes, Japanese sunken gardens, waterfalls, and forests of cottonwoods, hackberrys, and redbud trees. Geese, swans, quail, turkeys, and peacocks could be seen everywhere.

For the short time Lydie lived in the mansion, she enjoyed the palatial grandeur of her new home. She loved swimming in the cloverleaf swimming pool that was of Olympian size and strolling the Game Refuge's gardens and grounds. She also enjoyed launching a canoe from the Venice-styled boathouse and paddling about Whitemarsh lake with a flotilla of geese and swan in escort.

Lydie was intrigued with E.W.'s interest in fox hunting. Kennels and stables were built to house the best hunters E.W. could import. But fox hunting in Kay County was different than in the English countryside. John Joseph Mathews wrote, "Where the game of hunting has tradition, dignity, and taboos, especially in England, it would seem that each side—the hunters and the fox—knows the rules. But in the primitive Osage, where the coyotes chant to the moon and leave musk messages on limestone rocks, fence posts, and Geological Survey pins, the imported foxes knew something the huntsmen didn't know; that the coyotes of the Osage were warning the foxes to leave; they wouldn't allow them to encroach on their domain."

E.W. and Lydie lived in the mansion only two months after they returned from their honeymoon. They moved into the artist's studio because E.W. had virtually lost control of his company to J.P. Morgan and Company (Morgan).

E.W.'s relationship with banker J. Pierpont Morgan, Jr., had begun in 1924 when E.W. won Marland stockholders' approval to sell Morgan $12 million worth of Marland stock.

ABOVE: "The Hunt" was one of E.W. Marland's favorite paintings in the Marland Mansion. After Marland's death, Lydie entrusted the painting to Nan Sheets, longtime director of the Oklahoma Art Center in Oklahoma City. The painting was later returned to the Marland Mansion.

One of the reasons that insiders worried about Morgan taking control as the "bankers" of Marland was that financial agreements with Morgan allowed its designees to serve on the Marland Oil Company board of directors. After the first sale of stock to Morgan, George Whitney, one of the Morgan partners, W.C. Potter, president of Guaranty Trust Company of New York, and Charles F. Smithers, president of an investment banking house, were added to the Marland board which was comprised of E.W.'s young men who headed various departments in the company and a few large shareholders.

Whitney and Potter soon sold E.W. on the idea that the entire 15-member board, 12 of whom lived in Ponca City, need not always come to New York City for board meetings. Instead, an executive committee, three of whom were from the Morgan ranks and three from Marland Oil's organization, began exerting control over the Marland Oil Company operations.

By 1926, E.W. became aware, although he was hesitant to admit it to others, that he was losing control of the beloved company he had raised from infancy.

When newspapers claimed that the discovery of oil in the Los Angeles Basin, in the Seal Beach field, would make Marland Oil the greatest independent oil company on earth, E.W. was naturally buoyed, still he continued to worry that the Morgan interests were arrayed against him, that they were attempting to squeeze him out of power. Some of his own men tried to warn him of the Morgan intrigue, but in a show of optimistic pretext, he downplayed their concerns. "Things will work out!" he said.

However, in his essay, *My Experience With the Money Trust*, written in the 1930s, E.W. reflected on the dominance of the Morgan members of the executive committee that controlled day-to-day operations of Marland Oil:

The Morgan influence became supreme—and the builders of the Company lost control of its policy direction. Our former policy of developing and selling oil properties to finance company extensions was abandoned at the suggestion of the Morgan group.

They said there was no further need for us to finance ourselves in that way, that if a property was good enough for one of the major companies to buy, it was good enough for us to keep.

E.W. Marland brought fox hunting, with its English formalities, to Ponca City.

Seldom did the Morgan people on the executive board pay heed to E.W.'s proposals. His plan to sell the company's Kettleman Hills properties for $50 million was vetoed. Also snubbed was E.W.'s proposal to build pipelines that would transport west Texas production to the Gulf of Mexico and Permian Basin oil from New Mexico to the Mississippi River.

The second veto angered E.W. whose gut told him his company was slipping from his grasp. When the executive committee questioned him about how large an oil company should be, he knew his answer that "an oil company should never be larger than the vision of one man," sounded the end of his influence. He later wrote, "This answer of mine to their question marked the beginning of the end of my usefulness to them."

E.W. had tried to use the construction of the Marland Mansion to take his mind off his power struggle with the executive committee in New York City. It was rumored that he tried to sell Marland Oil for $59 million to Dutch Shell, if Dutch Shell would allow Marland Oil's operations in Ponca City to remain essentially intact. The Morgan people, regardless, vetoed the sale.

E.W. had basic disagreements with the Morgan partners. He believed they were misguided in thinking that the cure for the petroleum industry could be found in mergers and consolidations. He said, "They do not fear the evils that will result from the concentration of power in huge industrial units, and they do not fear the resulting destruction of individual industrial opportunity."

Time after time, E.W.'s plans of proposing new drilling programs and construction of pipelines were rejected by the executive committee. He knew the committee was not rejecting capital extension of pipelines because of any shortage of money in the company. When he was turned down on a Mississippi River pipeline proposal, the books of Marland Oil showed the company had more than $20 million in cash in government bonds deposited with Morgan banks.

E.W. saw what the New York bankers were doing. When $30 million of Marland Oil bonds were sold, the company had to borrow more money to operate. The Morgan interests made money on the commission of the sale of bonds and kept the money in their banks at a time when money rates were high. Marland Oil gained no benefit from the money—it could loan the money or invest it. Only the banks showed profit from the deal.

E.W. was concerned that even though he was president of Marland Oil, and knew its properties "like the back of his hand," decisions regarding the company were being made by men who spent two or three hours in a board room in Manhattan each month.

In the spring of 1928, E.W. had a conversation in New York City with W.C. Potter at which he asked if the executive committee had lost confidence in his leadership of Marland Oil.

In what would be the only criticism E.W. ever heard of his management, Potter said the executive committee thought E.W. was too cordial with his junior officers, showed too much human interest in his employees, and that officers should not be directors of the company. Potter said Marland Oil needed to have a president who would be "hard-boiled" and "two-fisted" in handling company employees. It was suggested that a new president be found and that E.W. be appointed as chairman of the board.

When E.W. advised his board of his meeting with Potter, three long-time directors, J.S. Alcorn, J.K. Cleary, and S.R. Sheldon, voluntarily resigned from the board and the company. They found their position both vulnerable and intolerable.

In June, 1928, E.W. appointed C.C. Brown as vice president and general manager of the company, proposing to the Morgan people that he would recommend that either Brown or General Baird Markham succeed him as president. The Morgan directors rejected E.W.'s proposals. They had already talked to D.J. Moran, a vice president of Texaco, who had agreed to take the job. The Morgan directors suggested that E.W. offer the job to Moran. Even though E.W. was officially making the offer, the deal had already been made behind his back. Moran promised E.W. that he would make no radical changes in positions at the top of Marland Oil management.

Immediately, E.W. was convinced that it was the intention of the executive committee to supplant him entirely in the operational management of Marland Oil. E.W.'s feeling was correct. Moran told the executive committee that it would be impossible to govern the company if E.W. lived in the same town where the company was located, or for that matter even remained with the company. Moran feared that his subordinates would appeal his decisions to E.W. if he was to remain as chairman of the board and that his presence would create an erosive environment within the new organization.

While at an executive board meeting in New York City, E.W. resigned as chairman of the board in November, 1928. Senior Vice President W.H. McFadden also submitted his resignation. It was not a spur-of-the-moment decision. Before they arrived in New York City, E.W. and McFadden had considered their options.

Other associates of E.W. probably should have resigned because within days Moran instituted a program of wholesale firing of longtime managers and superintendents of Marland Oil divisions and departments. E.W. wrote, "Scores of men who had given the best years of their lives to the upbuilding of the company were called in from the fields and

E.W. Marland always dressed formally for fox hunts or horse events with boots, pants to the knees, a hunting coat, and a sober face.

THE TAKEOVER   83

plants and were discharged without the slightest notice of consideration."

E.W. did not personally blame Moran for his actions. He knew Moran was following instructions of the banker management in New York City.

With E.W. out of control of Marland Oil, the company was merged with Continental Oil Company (Conoco) on July 1, 1929, and continued under the name of the latter company. There were 2,294 Conoco retail stations in 28 states and the District of Columbia. The new company maintained central offices in both Ponca City and Denver, Colorado.

At the time E.W. resigned as president and chairman of Marland Oil, he owed the federal government $3.2 million in back taxes. He and his lawyers had concluded he did not owe the taxes, but lost appeals for a reduction in the levy. He used $1.7 million cash and borrowed $1.5 million from Morgan to pay the government. He later said he should have sold stock to pay the government, rather than borrow money. The stock would later lose most of its value in the Great Depression.

LEFT: E.W. and Lydie Marland, portrayed by Mike Mott and Jayne Detten, at the west entrance to the mansion. The 1927 LaSalle for the modern photograph was provided by Ken and Yvonne Holmes and J.D. Hanks. *Courtesy M.A. Crank.*

Soon after E.W. Marland resigned as president of Marland Oil Company, the name of Marland Oil gave way to Conoco.

E.W. attempted to form new companies in 1929, 1931, and 1939, but had difficulty raising money, although some of his friends and former employees such as John Hale, John Alcorn, Gene Waldo, G.W. Blackard, Charlie Brown, Alex McCoy, H.L. McCracken, and George Roberts Marland agreed to join him in the ventures.

All of E.W.'s private land holdings, except the Marland Mansion and 37 acres around it, were incorporated into one holding company. But the Great Depression and the collapse of E.W.'s lines of credit caused his luck to simply run out. He only drilled one other well in his lifetime—and it was a dry hole.

When it appeared E.W. would be able to use his real estate holdings in Ponca City and a cotton plantation in Mississippi as collateral to pay off his debts, the stock market crashed in October, 1929. The more than $5 million of real estate in Ponca City and the $750,000 Mississippi property lost great value because of the onset of the Great Depression.

As the name Marland was replaced with Conoco on thousands of red triangles on tank cars, filling stations, trucks, pump stations, and company-owned buildings across the United States, the old Marland Oil Company was a thing of the past. As E.W. said, "The House of Morgan had merged it out of existence."

THE TAKEOVER

Governor Marland

E.W. REACTED to the Great Depression in the way that many Americans did. They cut back and used saved funds to live on. There was no money available to nourish his new ideas of re-creating the wealth he enjoyed at the helm of Marland Oil Company.

He had set aside considerable funds for Lydie and George, but had to use the money to literally keep the utilities and taxes paid on the mansion. He was embarrassed by the fact he could not come up with the final payments on the Pioneer Woman Statue. However, Lew Wentz came forward with the necessary money and Governor William J. Holloway declared April 22, 1930, a state holiday when the statue was dedicated.

By 1931 E.W. could not pay his debts and the holder of the mortgage on the Marland Mansion foreclosed. At a sheriff's sale on August 11, 1931, W.H. McFadden was the highest bidder, and for the sake of friendship, conveyed the property to E.W. Both men had no doubt that someday when E.W. got back on his feet he would be able to reimburse McFadden in full for his kindness.

E.W. turned his attention to politics in 1932. When Democrats suggested he run for the Oklahoma Eighth District congressional post, he said, "If they wish to nominate me, I will accept. But I am not announcing my candidacy for the position."

The Kay County Democratic organization endorsed E.W. for the Eighth District. He accepted the gauntlet and began campaigning. He used his own experiences of battles with the money trusts of the East and the federal government to try to identify with the people. He promised tax reform and to do what he could in Congress to destroy the money trusts which he blamed for losing control of his own company. He accused Republican President Herbert Hoover of being more interested in faraway Europe than "the good and virtuous people of the plains."

In the July 5, 1932, Democratic primary, E.W. defeated opponents F.L. Vaughan and Phil C. Ferguson without a runoff. With the Democratic nomination in hand, he launched his general election campaign against the Republican incumbent, Congressman Milton C. Garber of Enid.

At first hesitant to identify with the Democratic presidential nominee, Franklin D. Roosevelt, E.W. changed his mind when he heard Roosevelt speak on the radio. E.W. had called himself an "Oklahoma Democrat," attempting to separate himself from the national Democratic platform. However, even in the Republican Eighth District of Oklahoma, Roosevelt was inspiring confidence as people suffering the ravages of the Great Depression looked for a leader who could give them relief.

Joining forces with Roosevelt, E.W. carried his message against big government and big money to the people of the Eighth District whose boundary was practically the same as the old Cherokee Strip. In the general election on November 8, 1932, E.W. soundly defeated the incumbent congressman, 51,404 to 31,677. Two independent candidates received less than 800 votes. E.W. was the first Democrat elected in the Eighth District.

E.W. was convinced he was an authentic gentleman-statesman. He called his win a "sweeping victory." He had no certain plans but had the time to devote his entire agenda to the people. In the nation's capital, he took his predecessor's place on the Committee on Interstate Commerce. Other congressmen accepted him as an authority on the petroleum business. E.W. felt a kinship with Roosevelt who had been elected president.

John Hale, E.W.'s former secretary who had stayed with his boss even when he could not be paid, went to Washington, D.C. as a staff member. Hale helped E.W. draft speeches in support of Roosevelt's New Deal legislation that was intended to help Americans remove themselves from the clutches of the Great Depression. However, in the back of his mind, E.W. worried about giving the government too much power to regulate commerce, especially the oil industry.

E.W. endorsed legislation to restrict activities of banking interests and was particularly interested in bills that compelled conservation of the nation's natural resources. He preached that subsistence housing, which he provided for his employees in Ponca City, was one solution to the economic problems of the less fortunate of America.

In the autumn of 1933, E.W. decided to forego running for reelection as congressman from Oklahoma's Eighth District—instead, he wanted to be governor of Oklahoma. He told the House of Representatives in his farewell speech he would seek the office of governor of his adopted state "because the financial and economic situation of my state is so grave and requires the type of business leadership I feel that I can supply."

E.W. continued, "Oklahoma produced last year enough food for 10 times her own population but could not feed her own…We cannot abide famine in our land of abundance. If the people of Oklahoma will have me as their governor, I expect to give the rest of my public life in their service." E.W. was giving up certain reelection to his seat in Congress to try to help Oklahoma pull itself out of the Depression.

Monument to "The Pioneer Woman," erected at Ponca City and donated to the state of Oklahoma by E. W. Marland.

E.W. Marland used this brochure to promote his candidacy for governor of Oklahoma in 1934.

E.W.'s campaign for governor in 1934 was based upon the promise of bringing the New Deal to Oklahoma. His slogan was, "Elect Me and Bring the New Deal to Oklahoma." In the primary, he faced stiff opposition from 14 other Democrats, including Oklahoma House Speaker Tom Anglin of Holdenville. Anglin received the endorsement of incumbent Governor William H. "Alfalfa Bill" Murray.

However, in the July 3 primary, E.W. polled more than 50,000 votes over his closet competitor, Anglin. The two were pitted for a July 24 runoff until Anglin withdrew, saying it would be better for the Democratic party and for the state if he stepped aside and allowed E.W. to have the Democratic nomination.

E.W. turned his attention to the Republican nominee for governor, former United States Senator William B. Pine. E.W. traveled the state, promising to work with the national recovery program of President Roosevelt and to solve the huge unemployment problem in Oklahoma. He also promised to put into effect a businesslike administration that used sound economic principles to manage state government.

RIGHT: An empty canoe in a half-filled lake on the Marland Estate symbolized the condition of the estate just a few years after E.W. and Lydie vacated the main house and left the meticulously groomed grounds to return to nature.

Surprisingly, E.W. took very little criticism for his marriage to Lydie. His opponents tried to impugn his character by questioning his leases of school lands and attempted to paint him as a rich oil tycoon who did not care for the little man. Most of the time, all E.W. had to do was to remind voters that he himself had suffered greatly in the Depression and could identify with their woes.

During July and August, 1934, *The Oklahoma City Times* ran a series of articles about E.W. Reporter Harold L. Mueller wrote 18 chapters of what he called "The Story of E.W. Marland." The series was a huge boost to E.W.'s popularity in the state. In the last installment of the series, Mueller described his interviews with E.W.:

He is not an actor as are so many in public life. He does not dramatize, over-emphasize, or slide over any of the events that have checkered his years. I half expected, although I had been told otherwise, that I would find an undertone of bitterness in his recital when he told of the swift decimation of his immense fortune. Which meant that I was completely unprepared for the impersonal manner in which he related the rapid loss of more than $30 million.

From the matter-of-fact way in which he talked about huge income and staggering losses and the contrastingly enthusiastic way in which he told of what he did with his millions when he had them, I am certain he experienced more real joy when he established a park than when he closed a profitable deal;

that he felt more disappointment when a lieutenant failed him than when he lost a million.

He was prodigal with his wealth and I know he enjoyed giving it away. His interest in art is genuine, not assumed. His love of beauty, of growing things, of animals is real, not a pose. One has only to look at the home he planned, the landscaped grounds upon which it sits, and the plants and trees he has assembled there to know that they satisfy an honest hunger.

When the reporter asked E.W. if he thought he would ever live in the Marland Mansion again, E.W. answered, "No, I think not. Sometimes Mrs. Marland and I think we would not want to. There is a lot of responsibility about living in a big house. It is a lot of trouble. After the newness has worn off, there is nothing to it but care. We would rather put the place to some useful purpose."

E.W. was probably hiding his feelings about the house. He certainly enjoyed building it, but financial ruin did not allow him to ever enjoy living in the mansion. His longtime lieutenant and friend, John K. Cleary, who knew E.W. so well, said, "Neither E.W. nor Lydie ever enjoyed the big house. After 1928, it was an albatross hung around his neck. For three years, it was the Emperor's Castle and from then on, there was little glory and little pleasure in its possession."

Oklahoma voters liked E.W.'s message of hope for jobs and better times and elected him governor by more than 120,000 votes over Pine in the general election on November 6, 1934. Knowing he would need the help of the state legislature to enact programs to assist in the state's economic recovery, E.W. met with House Speaker Leon C. "Red" Phillips of Okemah and State Senate President Pro Tempore Claud Briggs of Wilburton before his official term began. The meeting took place at the Marland Mansion and was cordial. E.W. laid out his basic proposals and asked the legislative leaders for their support.

Crowds jammed the sidewalk as E.W. and Lydie appeared in a gala inaugural parade on January 15, 1935. E.W.'s longtime friend and co-worker, W.H. McFadden, rode a handsome horse from the 101 Ranch as grand marshal of the parade. The Oklahoma Military Academy band played patriotic music in advance of E.W.'s car.

Lydie, as first lady, was popular with Capitol photographers. On inauguration day, she happily posed in a beautiful gown on the stairs of the governor's mansion. That evening, dressed in a backless, velvet gown, she hosted a State Capitol

ABOVE: The souvenir inaugural program of E.W. Marland's inauguration as governor in January, 1935.

LEFT: Lydie Marland arrives at the governor's mansion in Oklahoma City in January, 1935, to assume her role as first lady of Oklahoma. *Courtesy Oklahoma Publishing Company.*

RIGHT: Princess Lydie, as many Oklahomans called her, poses on the spiral staircase of the Oklahoma governor's mansion on her husband's inaugural day in January, 1935. *Courtesy Oklahoma Publishing Company.*

party for thousands of men in tails and top hats and women in sequins. An air of aristocracy had returned to the governor's office after four years of Alfalfa Bill Murray's eccentric rule. E.W.'s top hat was in stark contrast to Murray's falling socks and old muffler worn at the inauguration four years before.

E.W.'s theme of helping the less fortunate had made it to the ears of Oklahomans. In the inaugural crowd were signs that read, "Poverty Must Be Wiped Out," and "Those Who Till the Land Should Own It."

John Joseph Mathews called E.W.'s inauguration day his "climax:"

That is, this date seemed to him to mark a climax, but in fact it was only a brief hour of illusion in his anticlimax. He had been the little god of the Outlet, now he was the little god of the whole Red Bed plains, of the woodlands, the pine-covered mountains, the canyons of live water in the Cherokee hills, the short-grass country, and the swamps of the southeast where the white heron nested.

Just as he had been the executive lord of a great oil company during a time when all men were loyal, from tool dresser to vice president, when his word had been eagerly accepted as law by thousands of people, so now he would be the beloved chief executive of a state.

In his inaugural address, E.W. warned citizens that tax increases would be certain if Oklahoma was to help its own. He promised that every effort would be made to assure an equitable distribution of the coming tax burden.

In presenting his plan to a joint session of the state legislature the following day, E.W. announced he had formed committees to study government and had contracted with the Brookings Institution to advise the committees. He suggested that massive unemployment in the Sooner State was the greatest task faced by the people and his administration.

In addition to recommending the passage of emergency legislation to assist in economic recovery, E.W. proposed the establishment of several new state agencies and commissions to deal with problems such as flood control, industrial development, and highway construction.

To finance the operation of a highway board, E.W. proposed a one cent gasoline tax. A severance tax on crude oil and natural gas would provide funds for other boards and agencies.

ABOVE: On weekends, Lydie and E.W. returned to Ponca City. In this photograph she tends to Red and Trotsky, the Marland's two Irish Setters.

LEFT: E.W. Marland's fraternity, Sigma Chi, featured him on the cover of a 1935 fraternity magazine.

BELOW: Governor Marland's Japanese gardener oversaw the planting of ivy to soften the wall of the governor's mansion in Oklahoma City. *Courtesy Oklahoma Historical Society.*

ABOVE: Lydie Marland was a popular first lady of Oklahoma with photographers. She seldom turned down requests for photo opportunities from photographers from the state's leading newspapers. *Courtesy Oklahoma Publishing Company.*

RIGHT: First Lady Lydie Marland appears at an art exhibit in Oklahoma City in 1936. *Courtesy Oklahoma Publishing Company.*

LEFT: Lydie's bedroom at the governor's mansion was furnished from furniture from the Marland Mansion in Ponca City. Now the bed is displayed with the same comforter at the Marland Mansion. *Courtesy Oklahoma Publishing Company.*

BELOW: The governor's mansion dining room during the E.W. Marland administration. On the buffet is the Marland silver service brought from the Marland Mansion in Ponca City. *Courtesy Oklahoma Publishing Company.*

LEFT: First Lady Lydie Marland in the library of the governor's mansion. Lydie was well read and accomplished in the social graces. *Courtesy Oklahoma Historical Society.*

BELOW: Governor Marland hosted a party for young Native American dancer, Yvonne Chouteau, in headdress. Chouteau later became one of the world's best known ballerinas.

Unfortunately, the legislature did not act on E.W.'s proposals as quickly as he would have preferred. After six weeks, the legislature had only passed a three-cent tax on cigarettes. E.W. personally appeared before a joint caucus of both houses and appealed for passage of emergency measures.

The slowness of the passage of the New Deal legislation could be attributed to House Speaker Phillips who opposed Roosevelt and New Deal programs. The cigar-chewing legislator said he wanted to help the destitute, but was moving slowly to protect the state "from the hallucinations of dreamers." Phillips was not as charitable as had been the free-spending E.W. during his heyday at Marland Oil Company.

E.W. used statewide radio speeches to condemn the legislature for its inaction. His campaign worked somewhat—the legislature finally passed a $2.5 million package for relief efforts, but just half of what E.W. had requested.

Much of E.W.'s legislative program was enacted into law during his four years in office.

Taxes on income, inheritances, cigarettes, and petroleum gross production provided additional sources of revenue for state government. New boards and commissions were also created. E.W. promoted the development of the Oklahoma Highway Patrol and the Interstate Oil and Gas Compact Commission.

While E.W. was governing, Lydie used decorating experience gained during the construction of the Marland Mansion to begin redecorating the governor's mansion. She carpeted the upstairs and moved many pieces of furniture and wall hangings from the mansion in Ponca City to the executive residence.

The governor's mansion's redecorated dining room was described in a 1936 newspaper story as "decorated in gold and green….Walnut paneling extends seven feet upon the walls around the room and tapestry is employed on the surface above."

Landscaping had always been important to E.W. who brought truckloads of magnificent shrubs and trees from the Marland Mansion grounds for use at the governor's mansion.

Oil was discovered beneath the State Capitol in 1935. E.W., with his vast experience in the petroleum industry, was the perfect man to be in the governor's office to develop the state's oil reserves.

Neighbors objected to E.W. allowing oil production on state property. However, E.W. won the legal and philosophical battle and

LEFT: Ernest Whitworth Marland, Oklahoma's tenth governor.

ABOVE: Governor Marland, center, hosted several of the nation's governors in the initial meeting of the Interstate Oil Compact Commission.

used the National Guard to protect drilling operations. The British American Oil Producing Company drilled the Pearson No. 1 well that produced 27,000 barrels in its first 24 hours.

E.W. and Lydie spent many weekends in Ponca City in the artist's studio where they had moved when he could no longer afford to live in the Marland Mansion. He was kind to job seekers and citizens who wanted to bend the ear of their governor. His old Ponca City friends came by to talk and swim.

E.W. was often seen strolling around the Marland Estate, but not usually alone. With him were John Hale, Gene Waldo, or Sam Collins. E.W. was invariably friendly, never indicating that children or visitors were unwelcome.

Once when E.W. and estate manager, Grover Blackard, were walking, they encountered young Bob Clark and his friends fishing in the south lake. E.W. asked, "How's the fishing?" Clark replied, "Swell. We've caught 11 perch, 4 catfish, and 2 bass so far."

The governor said, "That's a lot of fish, boys, but there are a lot more in there. What are you using for bait?" "Bacon and worms," was the reply. "Well, that's good bait," E.W. said, "but so are grasshoppers and I've got plenty of them around here. You better use some of my grasshoppers."

The Marland Mansion became a respite from the hassles of governing in Oklahoma City. When E.W. hosted meetings or political rallies at the Marland Estate, a steady stream of cars churned clouds of dust on the gravel roads, making fishing impossible when neighborhood children were sitting on a bank adjacent to the road.

While E.W. was visible to sightseers on the estate, Lydie was rarely seen walking the grounds. In 1937, she was attacked by a swan along the bank of Whitemarsh Lake and was required to carry her injured arm in a sling for a few days. Following the attack, E.W. ordered the swans removed from the property.

Both E.W. and Lydie extended invitations to friends to swim in the pool. Bob Clark's mother had been decorated with carved furniture, handsome pictures and books, and artistic masterpieces, were now bare. In rooms where luxurious beds had been covered with taffeta and silken covers, now stood saw horses with planks laid across them. Scum had formed around the huge swimming pool that had been the home to such gaiety and laughter in years past.

E.W. was not in good health. He suffered from the after effects of two slight strokes, one affecting his speech. Showing his age of 67, he talked with friends and visitors about people and places that had created his powerful and mystical presence on earth.

E.W. and Lydie had not been abandoned by their closest friends. Jane Clark, who E.W. had appointed to the State Board of Education, came often to see E.W., as did the Soldani girls and John and Corelia Hale. Often, E.W. lay in his bed listening to the chatter of friends who had come to see him. However, he was unable to speak due to a speech impairment caused by a small stroke. He was mentally alert and could listen to the conversations, but he could not join in because his vocal chords were paralyzed.

E.W. died on October 3, 1941. By his bed were Lydie, George Marland, his family doctor, Thomas McElroy, and a nurse. As E.W. took his last breath, he took Lydie's hand and whispered, "I love you more than anything in this world." There was never an official announcement of

RIGHT: Paul Prather with broken pieces of the Lydie Marland statue recovered in 1993. *Courtesy Oklahoma Publishing Company.*

the cause of death although E.W. suffered from stomach ulcers, respiratory problems, strokes, and angina from a blocked artery.

Bob Clark observed, "He passed away leaving scant indication, other than memorabilia, of the fabulous empire he once had built, the respect he had commanded, and the enormous wealth he could have, in a previous time, summoned at the beck of a finger. Yet his life and accomplishments were the stuff of legends, attestations to his uniqueness and consequence, proof of his greatness, yet sadly enough, evidence of his foibles. It was a story that should have ended on a happier note, or at least one that should not have left so many doubts or unanswered questions."

After a period of mourning, Lydie hired the law firm of Maris and Maris in Ponca City to probate her husband's estate that had dwindled from $100 million and control of a significant portion of the world's oil supplies to one automobile, a few items of art along with household furnishings, the chauffeur's quarters, and the use of the artist's cottage on the grounds of the Marland Mansion. Lydie chose to spell her name "Lyde" on the official papers asking that she be appointed executrix of the estate. A copy of E.W.'s simple, one-page will was attached to the Petition for Probate of Will. In the will, executed two years before, E.W. had left his entire estate to Lydie.

The beliefs of the monks who had purchased the Marland Mansion did not allow the presence of women, or statues of women on the premises. They requested that Lydie's statue be removed. For years the statue lay in weeds and brush next to the chauffeur's quarters into which Lydie had moved. In 1953, Lydie asked Glen "Gillie" Gilchrist, owner of a Ponca City monument company, to break the statue apart and "bury the pieces." Lydie never cared for the statue which in its forsaken and castaway state soon became an eyesore, even an object of loathing. "No one has a use for it," she told a friend.

However, Gilchrist did not have the heart to fully destroy the beautiful statue of Lydie. Though he hauled it off, he did not break the statue apart to the extent of Lydie's wishes. Instead, he buried the pieces on his company property. Forty years later, after Gilchrist's death and weeks before the property was to be laid over with concrete, a family member notified officials of the Marland Mansion of the statue's whereabouts. In 1993, the statue was recovered, reassembled, and refinished, and stands today in the mansion's foyer as though welcoming all who enter.

Lydie was 41 years old when her husband died. However, she looked younger than her age. Leading a lonely life caused her to slip deeper into eccentricity. Often she wore older clothing, some

Paul Prather admires the statue of Lydie Marland after it was pieced together in 1993. *Courtesy Oklahoma Publishing Company.*

of her wardrobe dating back to the 1920s. In conversations with friends, seldom did she refer to her husband as "E.W.," preferring instead to call him "Mr. Marland."

The years of hearing gossip about the circumstances of her marriage to E.W. had obviously taken their toll. She became even more private than before. Withdrawn from society, Lydie disappeared from the public view. She rarely left the chauffeur's quarters. Some people thought she had died—others assumed she was still traveling as she had often done in her first 30 years in Ponca City.

Where Lydie had amused herself with dogs and horses and luxury in the past, she was now forced by circumstances to live in a structure that had been built to house chauffeurs.

When Lydie needed funds, she sold pieces of art, although the once vast collection from Europe was greatly diminished because E.W. had sold many items to pay utilities and property taxes before his death.

In 1948, the Carmelite Fathers sold the Marland Estate to the Felician Sisters for $50,000. The sisters called their new home Assumption Villa, although townspeople still referred to the property as the Marland Mansion. The sisters built a chapel, a simple convent, and a two-story hall used for several years as a residence and high school for girls. Lydie had little to do with the nuns who occupied what she called "the big house" and spent their days in a highly disciplined regimen of prayer, reflection, preparing meals, and cleaning the massive property.

When C.D. Northcutt was president of the Ponca City Chamber of Commerce in 1950, he instigated an effort to move the large statue of E.W. that was lying in weeds on the Marland Estate to a prominent location in town. Northcutt appointed J.C. "Jake" Hampton as chairman of a committee that guided the program to place the statue on a fine granite base at the corner of Fifth Street and Grand Avenue in front of the Ponca City Civic Center.

Also in 1950, Lydie began a friendship with Louis Cassel, an army veteran and son of an oil-refinery fireman. Cassel was a meter reader for the Ponca City Water and Light Department who necessarily came close to Lydie's abode to make monthly electric meter readings.

At first, Cassel repaired broken appliances for Lydie and spent many evenings arranging her library and replacing light bulbs. Lydie, who desperately needed attention, began paying Cassel for his frequent trips to her quarters. Even Cassel's friends were invited for parties at Lydie's home.

Often, Lydie was seen with Cassel in his automobile heading on a motor trip, often with pieces of art in the back seat. Observers believed Lydie thought she could obtain higher prices for her treasures in distant cities.

Lydie's brother, George, his wife, Laverne, and their three children did not approve of Lydie's relationship. The disapproval caused many verbal skirmishes between the once close brother and sister. George often traveled from his home in Tulsa to caution his sister about spending all of her money on Cassel.

When Cassel grew tired of his companionship with Lydie, he stopped coming to her home. More than once Lydie hired private detectives to find him. Often, Cassel came back. In the summer of 1952, Lydie was able to accumulate $5,000 to buy Cassel a small wheat farm outside Ponca City. When Cassel sold the farm to satisfy a child support judgment from a previous marriage, he left town with a friend.

Lydie found Cassel, 19 years her junior, in Arizona and followed him. The former cab driver and soda jerk finally ended the relationship in a shouting match on Grand Avenue in downtown Ponca City.

It was the final straw for Lydie. In February, 1953, she packed her 1948 green Studebaker with her remaining pieces of art, a few tapestries, and $10,000 cash. George unsuccessfully pleaded with his sister to stay in Ponca City. But in the next days, Lydie left. George and Laverne would never see her again.

Lydie had never learned to drive and had never applied for a driver's license. Her vision was so faulty she had to use a magnifying glass to read a newspaper. Now, she was on her own, as she disappeared, no doubt trying to escape her very existence.

For the next 22 years, Lydie roamed America. Little is known except for bits of pieces of information developed from occasional letters and infrequent stories she later told to friends.

Lydie stopped in Arkansas City, Kansas to refuel. When people so close to Oklahoma recognized her, Lydie paid for the fuel and quickly left. At that moment she decided to lose her identity and never again be recognized as the former First Lady of Oklahoma.

Lydie was old news in Ponca City and no longer the topic of conversation. The Felician Sisters now occupied the mansion, the chauffeur's quarters lay silent and empty, and only memories remained of the once fabulous Marland Estate and those who had once dwelt there.

Occasionally, someone would relate stories of seeing Lydie working as a maid in a third-rate motel, the Moonlight Inn, in Independence, Missouri, or that she was seen standing in a breadline in New York City. No matter where she was, if she saw Oklahoma license plates on an approaching car, she hid like a fugitive. She painstakingly avoided anyone who knew her past.

In August, 1955, Lydie's brother, George, who was doing well in the oil and gas business in Tulsa, made a missing persons report to police. The Oklahoma State Bureau of Investigation entered the case. George waited two years to file the report because it had not been unlike his sister to disappear for long periods of time in the past without contacting him. Fearing foul play, George wanted answers. Unfortunately, no answers came before his death in Tulsa on January 19, 1957. George was only 59 years old. He left his interest in the gate house at the Marland Estate to Lydie.

Lydie's disappearance received national attention in 1958 when *The Saturday Evening Post* published a feature article titled "Where is Lyde Marland?" With photographs and more

UNITED STATES DEPARTMENT OF JUSTICE
FEDERAL BUREAU OF INVESTIGATION

WASHINGTON 25, D. C.

In Reply, Please Refer to
File No.

October 15, 1956

Mr. George R. Marland
1934 South Evanston
Tulsa, Oklahoma

Dear Mr. Marland:

Reference is made to my letter of July 12, 1956, regarding the missing person notice maintained in our files in your behalf since June, 1954, concerning Lyde R. Marland.

Inasmuch as no reply has been received to that letter, it is assumed that you are no longer interested in having Lyde R. Marland listed as missing. Therefore, unless advised by you to the contrary within thirty days from this date, the notice in our files will be cancelled.

Very truly yours,

J. E. Hoover

John Edgar Hoover
Director

Returned Letter as requested to F.B.I.
on November 3, 1956, stating Lyde still missing.

LEFT: In 1956, when Lydie had not been found by the Federal Bureau of Investigation (FBI), the agency's director, J. Edgar Hoover, wrote George Marland with news that the FBI file was being closed.

fiction than truth, John Kobler wrote a sordid story of Lydie's life and disappearance, an article that very much incensed E.W. and Lydie's friends who were still alive.

Following *The Saturday Evening Post* article, Robert Clark, Sr. wrote a letter to the author, criticizing the piece for its libelous tone. Kobler replied, saying that he had interviewed 40 people prior to writing the article. Clark asked all of the Marland's closest friends in Ponca City if they had been interviewed. Clark was not surprised that not one of the friends had been contacted by Kobler. "He made little effort to be objective," Clark said.

Most people who knew the Marlands believed that Kobler had from the outset intended to do a "hatchet job" on E.W. and Lydie, although no one knew what could have motivated the writer, other than the need for scandalous allegations to "spice up" the story and sell copies.

By 1956, Oklahoma authorities completed their investigation. Finding no evidence of foul play, the crime bureau file was closed. Agent Sid Wilson said, "We've uncovered no evidence of a crime, and if Mrs. Marland chooses to hide, I guess she's got the right."

In 1960, when Oklahoma law would have allowed Lydie to be officially declared dead, new developments arose. Her Studebaker convertible was found in a junkyard in Macon, Missouri. She had sold the car only a few months after she left Ponca City.

Several reporters who were dedicated to finding evidence of Lydie's whereabouts fed police information. The sheriff's office in Ponca

LEFT: "Where is Lyde Marland?" appeared on the cover of one of the nation's most popular magazines in 1958.

City uncovered conclusive proof that Lydie was alive and had lived in an apartment complex in California until late 1959. Lydie also was tracked to a post office box in Kansas City, Missouri.

For many of the years she was missing from Ponca City, Lydie maintained a passbook savings account at City National Bank and Trust Company in Kansas City. The initial deposit of $4,550, from the sale of a bond, was made in February, 1960. In her own hand, Lydie made notations that a March 1, 1960 deposit of $8,000 was from the sale of a painting. In August of that year, she noted that a $5,000 deposit was proceeds from the sale of a ring.

Withdrawals from the savings account averaged $500 a month in 1962 with few deposits except for interest earned. From 1965 to 1970, there was no activity in the account that had dwindled to $80.39. However, Lydie must have reappeared in the Kansas City area to deposit more than $6,000 into the account on April 15, 1970. Subsequent withdrawals depleted the account to $383.21 by February, 1972. Lydie never withdrew the balance.

Throughout the years, Lydie kept her property taxes paid on the small parcel of land she retained in Ponca City on the grounds of the Marland Estate. Each year, the county treasurer's office would receive a money order or cashier's check that usually was a few dollars more than the taxes. A deputy treasurer always placed the surplus money in an envelope with Lydie's name on it. The money was never claimed.

Lydie's whereabouts were not unknown to everyone. Her brother, Marland Roberts, who lived in Edmonds, Washington, kept track of her. Helen and Connie Cleary ran into Lydie in Kansas City in 1958. Robert Clark, Sr. contacted her in 1961 through her brother, Marland, and Lydie's New York City attorney. Grover Blackard, the longtime manager of the Marland Estate, heard from Lydie or about her on occasion. And it was said her family in Pennsylvania knew of her whereabouts.

In the 1960s, occasional reports reached Ponca City that Lydie had been spotted taking part in anti-war demonstrations in Washington, D.C. Such reports caused Ruth Blackard, the widow of Grover Blackard, to want Lydie found.

After the death of her husband, who some people called the last man to stay with E.W. through his bad days at the end of Marland Oil Company, Mrs. Blackard, affectionately called "Mrs B.," hired attorney C.D. Northcutt to probate her husband's estate. Mrs. B was a recluse and required Northcutt to check on her—she had a horror of being found dead on the floor of her home. She lived on a portion of the old Marland Estate. After the property was divided, her husband bought 80 acres and developed the Blackard Addition.

On one visit to Mrs. B's house in 1972, the elderly widow was concerned that Lydie's house was in bad shape. Vines were growing through the roof. Errant children with BB guns had shot out windows. Mrs. B told her attorney, "You must find Lydie and tell her we've got to do something about her house." Northcutt said, "What makes you think I can find Lydie when *The Saturday Evening Post* could not find her 25 years ago?" Mrs. B replied, "You're a lawyer aren't you? Find her."

Northcutt went to work, and eventually found a trace of Lydie at an address at Thomas Cook and Son, Inc, a travel agency on Fifteenth Street, N.W., in Washington, D.C. A letter to Lydie was sent, explaining the dilapidated condition of her house and the dire need of repair. There was no reply, but Mrs. B insisted that Northcutt continue his efforts.

Northcutt and Mrs. B inspected Lydie's home. They obtained a key from Felix Duvall, an attorney who had purchased the stables across the patio from Lydie's cottage. The stables had been converted into a beautiful home.

Massive cobwebs hung from the ceiling. Northcutt used a broomstick to slice through the cobwebs so they could enter the cottage. Ceilings were sagging because of extensive water damage. A musty odor permeated the structure. In the adjoining five-car garage were found a portrait of E.W., a large set of bookcases with glass doors, and the oil painting of Lydie in Spanish costume.

In early 1975, the Felician Sisters announced they would be leaving Ponca City to relocate in New Mexico. With the fact looming that the Marland Estate would again be on the auction block, Mrs. B asked Northcutt to hasten his efforts to find Lydie. He wrote another letter.

A few weeks later, Northcutt's receptionist buzzed him with the news that a Mrs. Marland was on the telephone with a collect call. He immediately took the call and a pleasant voice said, "This is Lyde Marland. I received your letter and it was chatty and friendly, I thought

I should call you and talk with you. I am thinking of coming home."

In a historic conversation, Lydie told Northcutt that she was in Washington, D.C., where she had been living with the street people. Northcutt offered to send her an airline ticket to bring her home to Ponca City. Lydie said, "I'm not ready to come home right now. I need some time, but I will eventually come home."

Northcutt asked Lydie if she needed some money. After much discussion, he agreed to send Lydie $500. He went to Security Bank of Ponca City and swore a trusted employee of the bank, Phyllis Vines, to secrecy. The attorney obtained five $100 money orders and sent them to Lydie in the nation's capital.

After 22 years of mystery, Lydie Marland was coming home.

A sad photograph of Lydie appeared on the first page of the feature article in *The Saturday Evening Post* in November, 1958.

This governor's widow was last seen on a Midwestern highway in 1953. Is she alive? Is she in hiding? Here are the strange facts.

Where is Lyde Marland?

By John Kobler

This is how Mrs. Ernest Whitworth Marland appeared about three years befo so mysteriously. If Mrs. Marland fails to turn up by 1960, she will be decl

THE END OF AN ERA   111

The Homecoming

DURING THE NEXT FEW MONTHS, Lydie wrote a series of incredibly descriptive letters to Northcutt. She thanked him for the money, for paying her taxes, and for giving her a warm, "down home" feeling on the telephone. She said it was not indifference that had caused her to leave unopened the letters she received from people in Ponca City over the years, but there was "too much feeling" to reopen past wounds.

In her scribbled hand, Lydie tried to express her fear of returning to Ponca City. She said how she missed her husband and her brother, George. She wrote, "Making that first call to you, opening that can of worms, has changed me. Nobody could ever understand. I hope I won't be too great of a disappointment to you who has extended a very friendly hand."

Lydie related some of the horror of her previous years:

> *Twenty-two years ago, I had to leave my home in Ponca City. People moved in on my life, for less than noble reasons, and it has been a nightmare ever since, breaking me down physically in every way. The invasion of, and exploitation of, one's private life is being called "the new cannibalism," and it is, that "psychological cannibalism." I was never a "missing person." I have spent years trying to evade the relentless surveillance, and never succeeding.*

Some days, it appeared Lydie was ready to return. On a particularly good day, she wrote, "Some days I long to let it all go and let others unravel a tangled mess. It would be just one more way I failed E.W. and everyone who ever liked me (my brother). Nobody can make it alone. We need a partner." On other days, the gravity of her circumstances appeared to be overwhelming. In one letter, she said:

> *Staying here so long has been a terrible waste of strength, money, everything. But nausea, blinding headaches, weakness, the "gut" resistance to forcing one more step of the way back—to what is left of the responsibilities I ran out on—psychological blocks—the weight of indebtedness— imposing on your time and patience.*

Green Country Inn
3910 NOWATA ROAD
BARTLESVILLE, OKLAHOMA 74003
(918) 333-0710

Monday

C.D. The trip west ---- I'll spare you the details — Sometimes on bad days or bad nights, I think I may never make it to P.C.

Along the way (Hot Springs, Tulsa, & Bartlesville) I hunted for apts. --- <u>imp-ossible</u>, scarce, costly, not desirable —

I came here (above) today — after five days at The Palace Hotel down by the railroad tracks. I don't mind the railroad tracks, as I am sentimental about the Santa Fe railroad, also "The Rock Island Line" (which is about to fold, I read.) — it was the hotel etc. ~~Hotel~~ It's expensive here, but a little more re-laxing for a meeting, and after 4th class for so long, it was something better — or a straight jacket and

---

A handwritten letter from Lydie Marland to attorney C.D. Northcutt received in the weeks before Lydie decided to return to Ponca City.

C.D. Northcutt
200 Security Bank Bldg.
Ponca City, Okla.
1669   74601

Lydie's letters were filled with her continuing paranoia that people still were searching for her. She wrote:

I dread recognition everywhere, but using a phony name goes against the grain. I would just be another item for the files. The surveillance is not past history. It is known where I am now, and "they" will know. Hotels like this have many retired snoops… they enjoy their work, they know who you are, but you don't know who they are. Their one way eye glasses can see out but you can't see in. I hate them.

By the spring of 1975, it was apparent that Lydie was getting closer to coming home. From a hotel in Hot Springs, Arkansas, Lydie asked for another $100. Northcutt complied with her wish and sent $100 by Western Union to Lydie at the Marquette Hotel in Hot Springs.

Lydie worried about how Northcutt would respond to her condition. She was 75 years old, and wrote, "The nightmare of my life since I left there. I'm a humiliating physical wreck and dread seeing you. I have the impulse to keep putting it off. I can understand how you may regret getting involved. For years, to make money last, I've done without basic needs for well being and appearance."

Then, Lydie called again. This time, she was only a short distance from Ponca City, in room 38 of the Green Country Inn in Bartlesville, Oklahoma. Northcutt told Lydie, "I will be there within an hour to pick you up and bring you home."

With part of the $500 in money orders Northcutt had sent to Lydie in Washington, D.C., she had purchased a bus ticket and made her way to Bartlesville. But, she still was not ready to make the final journey to Ponca City. She told Northcutt, "I am not ready to come home right now. I need to have some more time." Northcutt replied, "Lydie, you are just like a honey bee circling a flower. You need to come home and be with your people."

After a short conversation, it was agreed that Northcutt would at least drive to Bartlesville and talk with Lydie in person. Northcutt drove through a heavy thunderstorm for most of the trip to Bartlesville. When he arrived at the Green Country Inn, the door to room 38 was standing wide open. "How strange!" he thought, "for Lydie Marland to have a door standing open."

He walked into the room and called out for Lydie. Then, he received the shock of his life.

From the bathroom walked a tiny woman whose wrinkled face was framed by iron gray hair. Her upper teeth were missing and two lower teeth were black with decay. She was wearing a black Chinese smock over pantaloons. The toes of her tennis shoes were worn through.

Lydie Marland, the once graceful and beautiful First Lady of Oklahoma, extended her hand to Northcutt. The attorney said, "No, Lyde!" and took her in his arms and held her, whispering, "Welcome home!"

With the storm approaching Bartlesville, Northcutt hurried Lydie from the room to the Hillcrest Country Club for dinner. He had called Carroll Rodman, the former assistant manager of the country club in Ponca City, to make reservations. Lydie protested, saying she would be a sorry dinner companion.

Northcutt let Lydie out under the country club portico and parked his car just before the heavens opened up to dump buckets of rain on Bartlesville. Inside, the two were shown to a private table. As Rodman, the manager of the country club, walked toward the table, Northcutt quickly asked Lydie her maiden name. When Rodman arrived at the table, Northcutt said, "Carroll, I want you to meet Mrs. Roberts who is with me today."

The waitresses could not keep their eyes off Lydie who appeared as a bag lady who had just walked in off the street. Northcutt asked Lydie if she wanted a cocktail. She said she had not had a drink in 20 years, but asked, "Do you think they have Dubonnet?" Luckily, the country club had a bottle of the fine wine that Lydie had grown to appreciate during her years as the princess of the Marland empire. She dipped a teaspoon into her glass of Dubonnet and sipped it, one teaspoon at a time. For dinner, she had a half peach with cottage cheese.

What followed was a titillating two hours of conversation with possibly the most mystical woman in Oklahoma history. Lydie related how she had hidden from public view for more than 20 years, that she was aware of the article in *The Saturday Evening Post*, and the resulting nationwide hunt for her. She said she had looked for an apartment along the way to Bartlesville, in Hot Springs, Arkansas, and Tulsa. She had stayed at the Palace Hotel in Bartlesville for five nights before moving to the Green Country Inn.

When Northcutt mentioned that a portrait of E.W. was now hanging in the lobby of the Security Bank in Ponca City, Lydie was angered into rebellious statements against all financial institutions, even the United States. Lydie said she would renounce her citizenship if she had some place to go.

After the pleasant dinner was concluded, Northcutt took Lydie back to the motel. She said she would call when she was ready to return to Ponca City. On his drive home, all Northcutt could think was, "What a complicated piece of human machinery!" With her transition from niece to daughter, wife, and First Lady of Oklahoma, surely Lydie's sensitive nerves were shattered.

The next time Northcutt heard from Lydie was a few weeks later when she telephoned from a home on Quail Lane in Ponca City. She had clandestinely taken a bus from Bartlesville to Ponca City and rented a room on the fourth floor of the Jens Marie Hotel. She had walked from the hotel to see her cottage a mile away and had become exhausted in front of a home on Quail Lane. Not knowing who she was, the occupants allowed her to call Northcutt.

When Northcutt arrived, Lydie was sitting on the curb in front of the house. He took her to his home where his wife prepared her a bowl of soup before she was returned to the Jens Marie Hotel.

Lydie's presence in Ponca City was a well-kept secret until Northcutt could put together a group of people who would provide money to repair her cottage. Lydie did not feel she was worthy of the effort, but Northcutt told her, "You are a national monument."

Lydie never drove again, and walked to a health food store and other businesses for as long as she could. Occasionally she might chat with someone if she initiated the conversation. However, if anyone recognized her and started a conversation, she would walk away and refuse to talk.

As Northcutt and Lydie became better acquainted, she revealed she had two suitcases of memorabilia and notes. Northcutt convinced her of the need to bring a recorder to tape an interview with her to establish for posterity some of the great history she had lived.

A few weeks later, Lydie summoned Northcutt to her hotel room and angrily accused him of revealing her whereabouts to a reporter for the *Tulsa World*. Northcutt had nothing to do with the story and Lydie believed his suggestion that possibly employees of the hotel had discovered her identity. However, the tape recorder idea was off and Lydie informed Northcutt she had destroyed the precious and invaluable two suitcases of memorabilia and notes.

Lydie's passion for privacy and her rebellion against what she thought might be intrusion into her life caused her in many ways to withdraw from the world. Once when Northcutt and a law partner had traveled to a suburb of St. Louis, Missouri, on a legal matter, Lydie was suspicious. When Northcutt returned, Lydie asked if he had been in St. Louis visiting her art dealer. When Northcutt assured her he was on legal business for another client, Lydie grew calm and they had a nice chat.

Northcutt remembered, "Lydie could be vivacious, interesting, communicative, and vibrant, but only when she felt she initiated conversation and only when she felt entirely at ease and confident."

From the Jens Marie Hotel, Lydie moved into a small apartment on South Fifth Street in Ponca City while her cottage was being repaired. Lydie placed aluminum foil over the windows to protect her privacy. In time, the cottage was updated and Conoco graciously provided Lydie a $1,000 a month pension as the widow of the founder of the company.

In the summer of 1975, taxpayers in Ponca City were asked to approve a two-year sales tax to raise $717,500, half the money needed for the city to purchase the Marland Mansion and surrounding property from the Felecian Sisters. Conoco pledged to match the revenue raised by the temporary sales tax. In support of the tax, Lydie wrote an open letter to the people of Ponca City. The letter was published in the *Ponca City News* on August 10, 1975:

I had not wanted to be involved in this matter, or to have anything to say about it—but in the past few weeks I have learned what the alternatives are, to the city owning this property—and I do believe that for the city to own it, is the best answer for ensuring the protection for the future of a structure that is unique—and also, I feel it would add to the many unusual and attractive features that makes Ponca City the outstanding city of its size, that it is.

I deeply regret that the Church is vacating the property. They have maintained it with dignity—with love and concern—and respect for the man who built it. A quiet refuge from the mad, mad world outside its walls.

My own feelings about the place are naturally emotional and personal—but I would like to say this much—to me it is a place of rare beauty and artistic integrity. A structure that is an expression from mind into substance, of the quality, the strength, and the heart of a man.

—Lydie Marland

On September 16, 1975, voters in Ponca City approved the temporary sales tax, allowing the city to buy the Marland Mansion and keep it in public hands forever.

The Marland Estate swimming pool during the time the property was owned by the Felecian Sisters. The pool was filled in the 1960s, but the border outline remains. *Courtesy Glenn Sanders*

ABOVE: Several new buildings were constructed around the Marland Mansion during the decades the property was owned by the Felician Sisters. *Courtesy Ponca City News.*

Settled in her cottage, Lydie became friendly with a small group of people. Larry and Virginia Stephenson developed a close friendship with Lydie. The Stephensons lived near the Marland Estate, a short distance for Lydie to walk and occasionally peck on their door. Larry was president of Security Bank, an institution founded by E.W. Possibly because of the connection, Lydie felt comfortable with Larry and Virginia. On one occasion when the three friends were having a glass of Sherry in the Stephenson living room, Lydie broke into giggles and said, "If some of my critics could see me now, they would say, 'Now she has become an alcoholic.'"

At the first Christmas after Lydie returned to Ponca City, employees of Security Bank filled a huge basket with fruit, nuts, and candies. When Larry delivered the basket, Lydie said, "Oh no, I don't take charity!" However, she was hungry and withdrew fruit from the basket before she commanded Larry to take the basket to "someone who really needs it."

Lydie shared with the Stephensons occasional glimpses into her past. She said that her life might have been different if E.W. and her brother, George, had not screened her romances so much. When a young man would arrive at the Marland home for a date with Lydie, he first had to be interviewed by E.W. and George. Lydie said, "It was enough to scare anyone off!" She related the story of falling in love with a French

THE HOMECOMING

count who, after his interview with E.W. and George, never appeared again.

Lydie conceded that E.W. and George were concerned about fortune hunters. At the end of many conversations, she said, "Oh, I miss my men so much!"

One day, Larry appeared at Northcutt's office with a check from Lydie for $1,500. She wanted to repay him for past loans. Larry and Lydie were mum about the source of the money, but Northcutt believed the City of Ponca City may have bought the full-length portrait of Lydie that now hangs in the Marland Mansion.

Another possible source of the money was a $20,000 check Lydie received from an art dealer in Santa Fe, New Mexico, who sold a painting Lydie had left with him many years before when she was traveling in anonymity around the country.

A person who spent a great deal of time with Lydie during her final years was Lana Lyons who had first met Lydie when she temporarily lived on Fifth Street while her cottage was being made ready for occupancy. Lyons cleaned Lydie's cottage. She found the once, elegant, well educated, and vibrant lady now a private, frail, and distrusting soul, living as a pauper.

Lydie's hands were always red and raw from constant washing in soap and water standing in a crock bowl in the sparsely-furnished kitchen. Lydie sat on a metal stool to take her sparse meals at a small chrome table. She wore clothing from the Salvation Army, saying she liked clothing that was soft from years of wear and washing. Lydie loved to ride in Lyons' Cadillac, often remarking, "Mr. Marland really liked Cadillacs!" Lyons often drove Lydie to Miller Market to buy groceries.

Lydie had a dime-sized dark mole that she always covered with a band aid at the base of her neck. She usually wore an apron and a faded red, white, and black paisley neckerchief as a bandana. Occasionally, she was seen with a pale green cloth raincoat, faded-pink nylon pajamas, or a tan raincoat with the sleeves rolled up.

LEFT: Originally the Marland stables, the structure became the private residence of Charles and Betty Thompson. *Courtesy Ponca City News.*

RIGHT: At the 1975 reopening of the Marland Mansion, are, left to right, Howard W. Blauvelt, Mayor Kenneth Holmes, Larry Stephenson, and John Robinson. *Courtesy Ponca City News.*

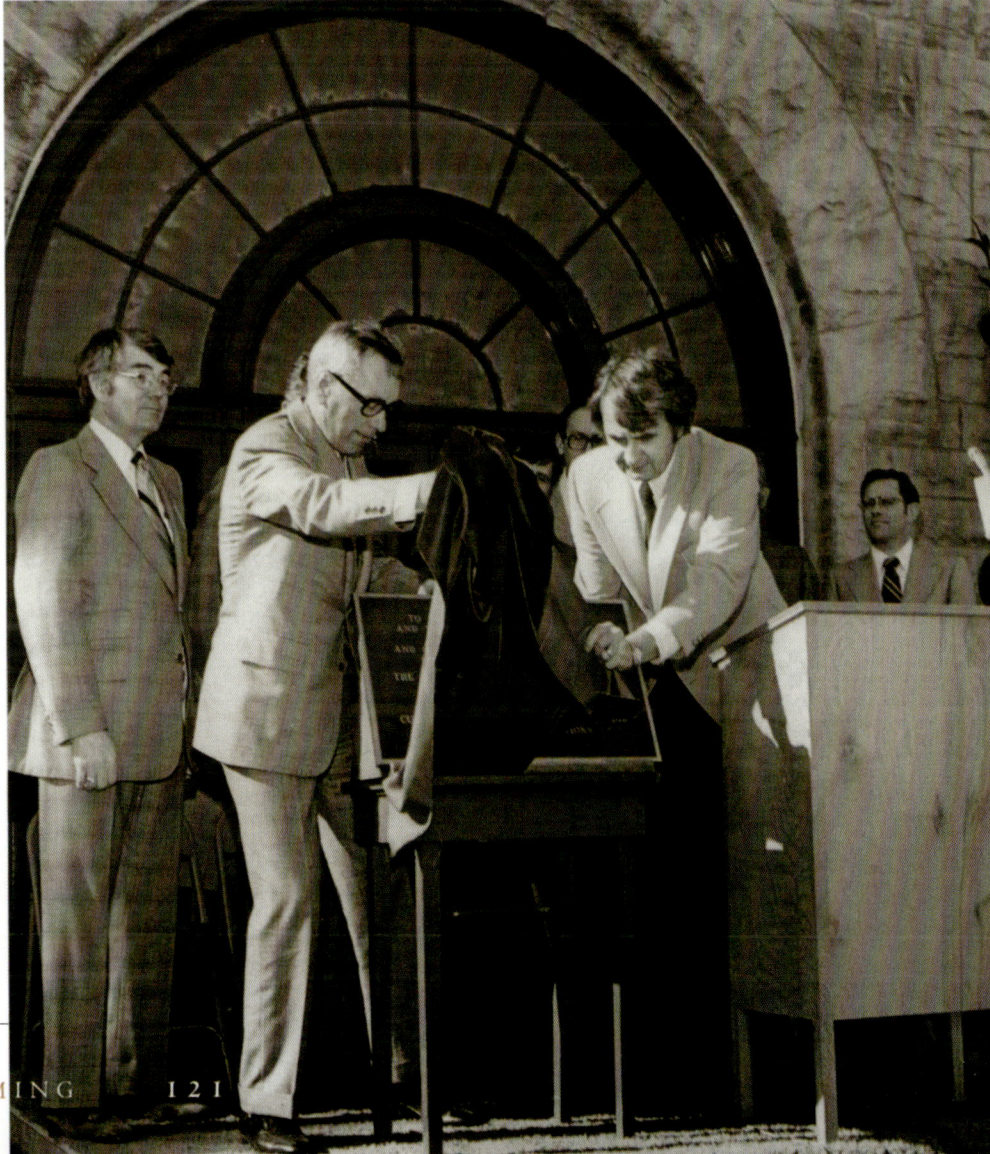

THE HOMECOMING 121

Occasionally, Lydie would come out of her sheltered existence. Once when Leslie Paris and Carol Walker passed Lydie in their automobile as she walked home, they offered her a ride. She shocked them by accepting, and slipped into the back seat. Lydie was inquisitive about disco dancing classes the girls were taking. She even invited Leslie and Carol into her home for a brief visit.

On another occasion, Lydie noticed that Leslie was walking by the Marland Mansion each day in a partial body cast. Leslie had undergone back surgery and walked for exercise in the neighborhood of her home that was located about a block from the mansion. Lydie invited Leslie inside the mansion gate and asked a series of questions about the accident and Leslie's classes at Oklahoma State University. "To see Lydie in her old, dark clothes and scarf was depressing," Paris remembered, "but it was exciting to hear her eloquent voice talk about 'worldly things' like literature and art."

LEFT: The original Marland Mansion and Estate Commission. Left to right, first row, Larry Stephenson, chairman, Dee Barrington, Allen Muchmore, and executive director Charles Hepler. Second row, Bob Westmoreland, Marion Jones, John Northcutt, and JoAnne Muchmore. Third row, John Carpenter, Jerry Brace, Billie French, and Madalynne Peel. Fourth row, Ron Duggins, Carolyn Renfro, Claude Brazier, and Gene Heagy. Back row, Fred Radd, Wanda Betow, and Prentice Hapgood. Not pictured were Evelyn Hunter and Maxine Warren. *Courtesy Ponca City News.*

Even though she was living in a past generation, Lydie never lost her love for art. Once when C.D. Northcutt was out of town, Lydie visited with his law partner, John Raley, who ushered the frail Lydie into his office. Suddenly, her pale and clouded eyes brightened as she fixed on a large oil painting on the wall behind Raley's desk. It was a John Warren painting of bluebonnets, live oak trees, and scrub mesquite, typical of the Texas Hill Country.

Lydie stood up and walked over to study the painting, commenting on the quality of the work. Raley remembered, "For a brief moment, in a stranger's law office, Lydie may have been transported back to a time in her youth when she was surrounded by gracious living and works of art."

The night was especially filled with fear for Lydie. Bill Hargraves, who owned a taxi service and security company in Ponca City, received a call one night asking for a security guard. Hargraves recognized Lydie's voice and said there would be no charge for him checking out the house. However, Lydie insisted on paying. The same attitude was present when Hargraves would see Lydie walking home from the shopping mall. Lydie refused a free ride, insisting on paying.

Hargraves became protective of Lydie. One morning, Lydie called him to report that someone had broken into her house the night before. Oddly, she was giggling as she said she knew someone was going to kill her. She insisted Hargraves come to the cottage to see what she was talking about. When he arrived, Lydie ushered him into the front room where obviously a raccoon had descended the chimney during the night, his soot-tracks marking his course through the room.

Hargrave knew his bounds with Lydie. He remembered, "She was a very private person. Her voice to me was like poetry or a song. She was one of the kindest ladies I've known. We used to talk and walk around the grounds of the estate. I knew just to listen and never ask questions. Sometimes, we said nothing. At times, she would reach for my hand to hold as we strolled. Her hands were so very tiny and pale. One could see her inner beauty through those intelligent but sad eyes. I can understand why Mr. Marland loved her."

Next door to Lydie lived Betty and Charles Thompson who had purchased the remodeled stables from Felix Duvall. The Thompsons and Lydie shared a love for cats. Lydie had a very independent cat she called "White Cat."

Lydie was painfully aware of events that were held at the Marland Mansion. In 1979, Ponca City native David Jones was producing and directing a one-act comedy at the mansion on a spot where the Felician Sisters had filled in the huge swimming pool with dirt. During a performance of the comedy, Jones was approached by Lydie, who had been tempted from her cottage to watch the performance.

Jones pulled off his coat and spread it on the ground for Lydie to sit and watch the comedy. Lydie asked him grueling questions about the performance and ended the conversation with an enchanting story about skinny-dipping in the pool many years before.

At the end of the performance, Jones walked Lydie home to her cottage. She asked him to remain outside a moment while she retrieved something. Lydie returned, kissed Jones on the cheek, and handed him $6 and a note that read, "My admission."

During concerts on the grounds, Lydie was often seen with a veil over her head sitting off in the distance, wanting to be private, yet wanting to hear the beautiful music that emanated from the artists. Sometimes, she could be seen near the gazebo dancing with an imaginary partner that only she could see.

In early 1987, Lydie expressed her wish that the City of Ponca City have her cottage after her death, a wish that surprised C.D. Northcutt because Lydie had always had a love-hate relationship with the town. Her idea was that Northcutt prepare a contract in which the city promised to pay $750 per month to Lydie until her death—then the city would own the property free and clear.

The contract was drawn and the city fathers approved an agreement to pay $10,000 cash and $750 per month. Unfortunately, Lydie collected only two monthly payments.

Near the end of her life, Lydie would often call Lana Lyons in the middle of the night. Lyons would answer the phone to no reply. Hearing Lydie breathing, Lyons would ask, "Mrs. Marland, is that you?" Lydie would always reply, "Yes, Lana, it's me. I just need to know that you're there."

The last time Lyons saw Lydie was when Lydie asked her to return some of her items

ABOVE: Reverend Ken Gates, pastor of Ponca City's First Presbyterian Church, presided over the very small funeral of Lydie Marland. *Courtesy Ponca City News.*

to the Salvation Army. Together, they sacked up black leather riding boots, a croquet set, clothing, the crock bowl that Lydie used in her kitchen, and a small plastic bag in which Lydie kept a small hammer, screwdriver, and miscellaneous tools.

Before C.D. Northcutt left Lydie's cottage for the final time, Lydie grabbed his hand and said, "C.D., I have something to tell you. You must promise you will never reveal it to anyone until after my death." She then said, "While E.W. was alive, he told me that he loved me more than anything in this world."

Within two weeks, Lydie was admitted to the hospital. When Northcutt visited her, she was weak and almost comatose, but would awaken long enough to look at him. But she did not speak.

On July 25, 1987, Lydie died at the age of 87. Only six persons attended her private funeral—Northcutt, who clutched the bundle of letters Lydie had written to him before her return; Florence and Gordon Holland, distant relatives of Lydie; Larry Stephenson; the funeral director; and Dr. G. Kenneth Gates, the minister.

However, a large congregation of Ponca City residents attended an August 6 memorial service in the Inner Lounge of the Marland Mansion. C.D. Northcutt and Rick Miller offered personal stories and tributes to Lydie. Gene Thomas, vice president of Conoco, paid tribute to the contributions of the Marlands to Ponca City and to Conoco:

A long chapter in the history of Conoco quietly came to a close…with the passing of Mrs. Lydie Marland. She was part of the Marland legacy which was started when E.W. Marland found oil just a few miles southwest of here…

Mrs. Marland was a quiet, private person. She was a proud person in the sense that she wanted to handle her own affairs and didn't want to bother others for help. As the wife of the former chairman of our company, she received a monthly annuity-type check from Conoco. I visited with her on a number of occasions—took her home from the grocery store—and offered my help and Conoco's help.

She was always gracious in her appreciation and periodically she would write a letter of thanks to Conoco. One Sunday about four years ago, she walked down to our house to bring one of the letters. We just lived a block away. We were not at home, so she stuck the letter in the door. It was a short letter, but the gist of it was, "I just want to say thank you."

In a front-page story, the *Ponca City News* said, "To the end, Lydie remained loyal to the memory of E.W., refusing to discuss her life with him…For the public, most will visualize Lydie dressed as Carmen in the painting hanging on the wall of the Ballroom of the Marland Mansion. Lydie is gone, but the mystique lingers on."

BELOW: Lydie's carriage, empty of the former First Lady of Oklahoma forever.

ABOVE: Conoco made significant contributions to the purchase and restoration of the Marland Estate. In this photograph, Conoco vice president Gene Thomas, right, welcomes Lydie Marland's brother, Marland Roberts, to the Conoco boardroom in 1987. *Courtesy Ponca City News.*

Return to Grandeur

SINCE THE CITY OF PONCA CITY took title to the Marland Mansion in 1975, a splendid effort has been made to restore the mansion to its original grandeur. The Marland Estate Commission and the Marland Estate Foundation have worked to raise money from private donors and government agencies to fund repairs and renovations to the mansion and the surrounding buildings and grounds.

E.W. Marland dreamed of living in a palace—and he built one on the prairie in Ponca City, Oklahoma. The National Historic Landmark is 78 feet wide and 184 feet long, and contains 43,561 square feet distributed over four levels. There are 55 rooms, including 10 bedrooms, 12 bathrooms, 7 fireplaces, and 3 kitchens. It takes 861 light bulbs to light the mansion.

LEFT: A large rock outside the west entrance to the Marland Mansion appropriately introduces visitors to the magnificent estate. *Courtesy Robert Burke.*

From the South Terrace, E.W. Marland could see the Pioneer Woman Statue and the top of his first home on Grand Avenue. *Courtesy Robert Burke.*

ABOVE: In 2001, many of the buildings added to the Marland Estate during the years of occupancy by a monastery and convent were removed. This photograph shows the chapel, Assumption Villa, being torn down. The chapel had been dedicated in 1963. *Courtesy William C. Ziegenhain.*

ABOVE: Visitors to the Marland Mansion are greeted with an imposing lobby. *Courtesy Robert Burke.*

RIGHT: Many historians believe the Marland Mansion is the greatest private home ever constructed in Oklahoma. This is the north terrace. *Courtesy Robert Burke.*

LEFT: Magnificent detail on windows and balconies add to the beauty of the South Terrace of the Marland Mansion. *Courtesy Robert Burke.*

RIGHT: A close-up of the corbels carved with flowers beneath the balcony on the south side of the mansion. *Courtesy Robert Burke.*

LEFT: Italian stone carver Pelligrini created the likenesses of E.W. Marland's four dogs under each corner of the porte cochere at the west entrance. Throughout the mansion are many examples of Marland's love for dogs and horses. *Courtesy Robert Burke.*

CENTER: The lead gutter boxes and drainpipes on the mansion were stamped with the letter "M." *Courtesy Robert Burke.*

ABOVE: Excess water collecting on the roof flowed from the mouth of Pan on the south wall of the mansion into a well below. *Courtesy Robert Burke.*

BELOW: The statues of Lydie Marland and her brother, George Marland, now stand in the lobby of the Marland Mansion. They were sculpted by Jo Davidson, E.W. Marland's favorite sculptor. *Courtesy Robert Burke.*

LEFT: Lydie's statue was restored by Dane L. Pryse and Zack Pryse, Jr. so perfectly that only a trained eye can see that the statute was once broken into many pieces at Lydie's direction. *Courtesy Robert Burke.*

Stone carver Pelligrini added two owls to welcome visitors to the gallery level of the mansion. In the background is a domed ceiling done in gold leaf mosaic, placed piece by piece by Italian artist Vincent Margliotti. *Courtesy M.A. Crank.*

LEFT: Throughout the mansion are custom-made ornamental iron doors, fixtures, and railings. The wrought iron was heated until it became flexible, then was shaped by hand. *Courtesy Robert Burke.*

The ceiling above the landing is a Margliotti masterpiece that is one of the Marland Mansion's true art treasures. *Courtesy Robert Burke.*

ABOVE: The service kitchen has no stove or oven because food was cooked in the main kitchen on the lower level and brought to this kitchen by dumbwaiter. Monel, a metal similar to stainless steel and originally used on battleships, was used in the service kitchen. E.W. Marland wanted the newest and best of everything, including a steam-powered dishwasher in the kitchen. *Courtesy Robert Burke.*

FAR LEFT: The wood for the formal dining room walls are of Pollard Oak, a very rare type of oak that was harvested with special permission from the royal forests of England. The carvings were done in Boston before the wood was packed in water for protection and shipped to Ponca City. The dining room can seat up to 20 for dinner. *Courtesy Robert Burke.*

LEFT: The dining room wall sconces are Sheffield plate, an unusual alloy of silver and copper. Cherubs adorn the sconces, an example of many displays of angels in the mansion. *Courtesy Robert Burke.*

BELOW: The Marland Mansion had one of the first elevators installed in Oklahoma. It is lined in buffalo leather and services all three floors of the mansion. The elevator operates as efficiently today as it did when it was installed in 1926. *Courtesy Robert Burke.*

The fireplace in Lydie's bedroom is carved from pink Italian imported marble and is the smallest and daintiest of the seven fireplaces in the mansion. *Courtesy Robert Burke.*

Lydie Marland's bedroom was decorated with exquisite wood work of hand carved borders and panels that meet at rounded corners. The bed is original, returned to the mansion from the governor's mansion after E.W. Marland completed his term as Oklahoma's tenth governor. *Courtesy Robert Burke.*

RIGHT: Above the fireplace in E.W. Marland's bedroom are carvings that show Marland's love for polo and the regalia of the sport. *Courtesy Robert Burke.*

BELOW: E.W. Marland's private bathroom contained one of the first saunas installed in the United States. The shower has nine ceramic nozzles. *Courtesy Robert Burke.*

Oak paneled walls highlight E.W. Marland's English Tudor bedroom. *Courtesy Robert Burke.*

LEFT: The current entrance to the house in the west *porte cochero* of the mansion. *Courtesy Robert Burke.*

RIGHT: E.W. Marland used his study to conduct business and greet visitors. The room also served as his headquarters in his political campaigns. Note the shells at the top of the bookcases, patterned after those in the oval office of the White House. In this modern photograph, the Marlands are portrayed by Mike Mott and Jayne Detten. *Courtesy M.A. Crank.*

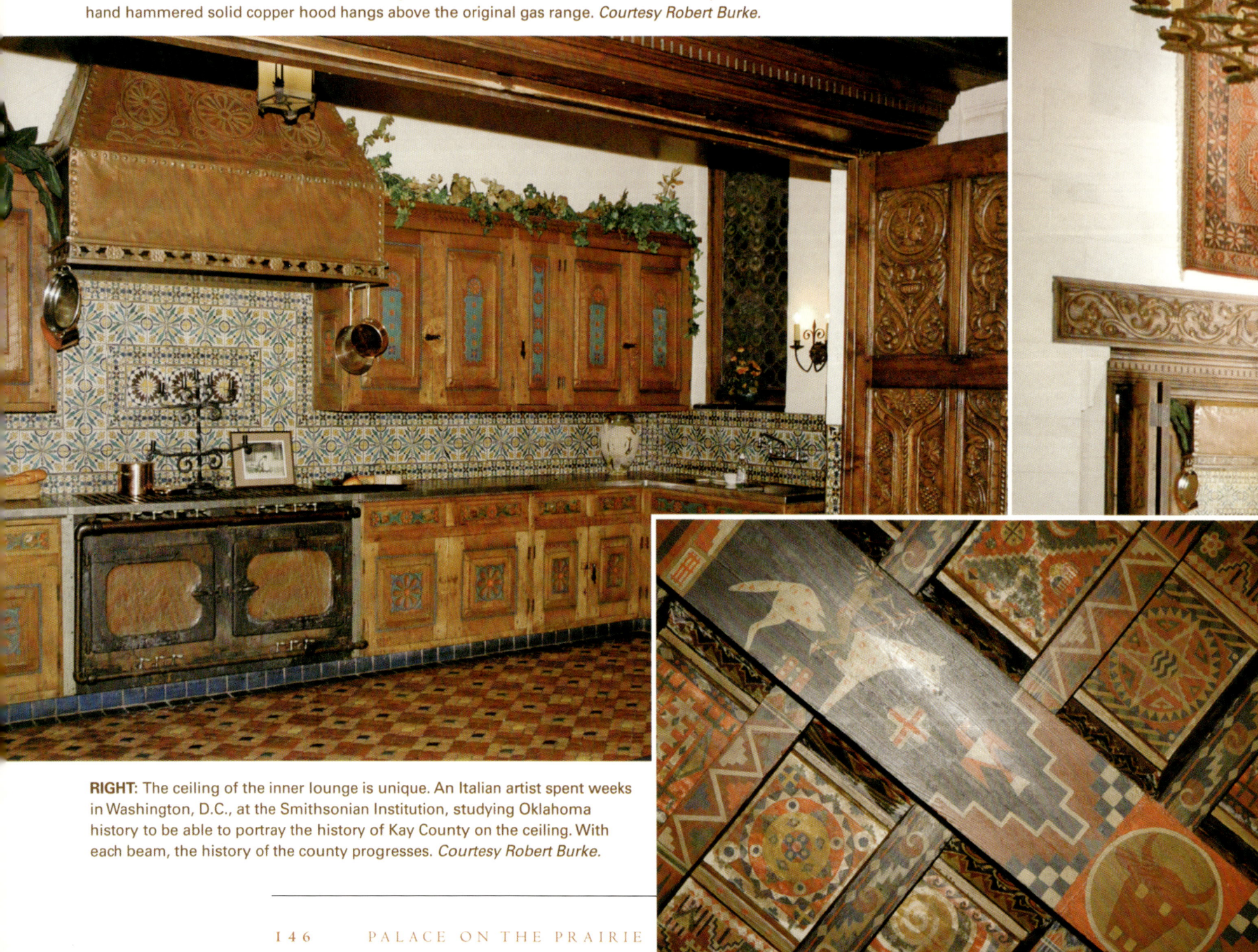

BELOW: The hunt kitchen, off the inner lounge, features hand carved cabinets and hand painted counter tiles. A hand hammered solid copper hood hangs above the original gas range. *Courtesy Robert Burke.*

RIGHT: The ceiling of the inner lounge is unique. An Italian artist spent weeks in Washington, D.C., at the Smithsonian Institution, studying Oklahoma history to be able to portray the history of Kay County on the ceiling. With each beam, the history of the county progresses. *Courtesy Robert Burke.*

The inner lounge was used as a gathering point for guests taking part in Marland's organized fox hunts. *Courtesy Robert Burke.*

RIGHT: E.W. Marland originally built the Artist Studio for his favorite sculptor, Jo Davidson. In the immense front room of the studio large windows and a skylight provide sufficient light for artists. Timbers from Marland's first oil well derricks form the vaulted ceiling and balcony. *Courtesy Robert Burke.*

BELOW: The bedroom of Lydie's Cottage where she lived the last 12 years of her life. Many original artifacts and memorabilia, in the Marland Family Exhibit in Lydie's Cottage, help portray the Marland family life. At left is Lydie's trunk used for world travel in her earlier days. *Courtesy Robert Burke.*

BELOW: The original chauffeur's quarters and garage (Lydie's Cottage) were remodeled into living quarters by E.W. Marland after his term as governor. He and Lydie made the 2,500-square-feet area their home and opened the mansion only for special events. The original building contained space for carriages and automobiles and quarters for chauffeurs. *Courtesy Robert Burke.*

RETURN TO GRANDEUR   149

ABOVE: The Marland Oil Museum on the estate grounds contains many artifacts of the rise to prominence of E.W. Marland and the Marland Oil Company. *Courtesy Robert Burke.*

BELOW: In the Bryant Baker Studio on the estate grounds is a collection of 44 plaster and bronze busts and maquettes created by the sculptor. After Baker's death in 1970, the City of Ponca City purchased the contents of his New York Studio and moved them to the estate. Among Baker's sculptures are those of John F. Kennedy, Winston Churchill, and Abraham Lincoln. *Courtesy Robert Burke.*

ABOVE: The south salon was used as a family room. It overlooked one of the most spectacular vistas of the estate. The floor of the salon is terrazzo, a compound of crushed marble and concrete. *Courtesy Robert Burke.*

LEFT: The palatial ballroom is lighted with antique Waterford crystal chandeliers with wrought iron bases imported from Ireland. Today's cost of replacing the ceiling and chandeliers in the ballroom is estimated at $2 million. *Courtesy M.A. Crank.*

LEFT: One of the most talked-about ceilings in the Marland Mansion is coated with 24kt gold leaf. Sheets of gold were hammered leaf thin and placed with adhesive onto the ceiling. E.W. Marland paid $80,000 for the gold for the ballroom ceiling. *Courtesy Robert Burke.*

ABOVE: On the gallery level landing is a unique ceiling treatment painted directly on the walnut panels in subdued colors, accented by a Lalique fluted crystal light fixture. *Courtesy Robert Burke.*

LEFT: Huge trees planted around the mansion nearly eight decades ago under the personal direction of E.W. Marland now obscure some views of the structure. *Courtesy Robert Burke.*

The Genealogy
OF THE MARLAND FAMILY

SINCE 1976 when the Marland Estate was formally opened to the public, many people have visited the estate to learn more about the E. W. Marland family. Some claim to be relatives. Anyone with the surname of Marland will try to establish or already know of his or her connection with E. W. Marland's family line.

Although not related in any way to anyone in the E.W. Marland family line. William C. "Bill" Ziegenhain, a resident of Ponca City, decided in 1997 to learn more about the family members of E. W. Marland, Lydie Marland, the Collins line, the Roberts line, and in particular the McLeod line of E.W. Marland's mother. This was done to satisfy a personal research challenge and also to determine if events could be found that helped to mold E. W. Marland's life into an oil empire builder and a visionary business leader who could foresee even in the 1920s that the wasteful production of oil and natural gas resources would eventually lead to serious economic problems in the nation and world.

The family member information already found would easily fill a book the size of this one. An easy way to at least present the names, relationships, and time periods involved is by using charts. Genealogists love charts. Following are eight selected charts to allow the patient reader a glimpse into the names of the family members in the selected family lines.

1. A 4-generation Ancestor Tree for
   Lydie Miller Roberts ....page 160
2. A 4-generation Ancestor Tree for
   Ernest Whitworth Marland ....page 159

The Ancestor Tree, also known as a Pedigree chart, lists the individual in the left hand column, the father in the box above and the mother in the box below. The four grandparents are then listed in the next boxes to the right of the parents and the great-grandparents are listed to their right. In addition to the names, only the year of birth and death is shown for each person. A blank in place of a date indicates the date is unknown. The Ancestor Tree chart is easily constructed and is a simple way to explain the persons involved in your own family history. The chart also readily points out the areas in which you need additional information

Following the Ancestor Trees for Lydie Miller Roberts and Ernest Whitworth Marland are six Outline Descendant Trees for the following family lines.

3. Outline Descendant Tree for
   George Marland, 1816-1892............. page 161

4. Outline Descendant Tree for
   Thomas Collins, 1810- ?.................. page 168

5. Outline Descendant Tree for
   John M. Fine, 1818-1878.................. page 171

6. Outline Descendant Tree for
   George W. Roberts, 1808- ?.............. page 164

7. Outline Descendant Tree for
   David McCloud(McLeod), 1810- ?.. page 166

8. Outline Descendant Tree for
   Sarah Ann McLeod, 1836-1905 .... page 173

The Outline Descendant Tree starts with the oldest person in the line and is designated with the number 1 to the left of the name. The children of number 1 are listed with a 2 to the left of their name. See the Outline Descendant Tree for George Marland (1816-1892) for an example, page 161.

The children of number 2 are listed as names with the number 3 to their left. This continues in descending order until all names are listed , A study of the charts, while confusing at first, will soon establish the correct way to interpret them. An alternate way of presenting the names by generation is to print a Descending Chart instead of the Outline format and charts several feet in width are produced. It was not practical to use that format for inclusion in the book.

In E. W. Marland's Ancestor tree we find the name George Marland, 1816-1892, which is the basis for the Outline Descendant Tree for George Marland.

We also find the name David McCloud, 1810-?, on the E. W. Marland Ancestor Tree which is also the basis for the Outline Descendant Tree.

In addition, the Outline Descendant Tree for Sarah Ann McLeod is included since her name is listed in two areas (1) the mother of E.W. Marland on the Marland Ancestor Tree and (2) as the mother of children with Henry Smith, 1831 -1867. This is only shown in her Outline Descendant Tree.

In Lydie Miller Roberts Ancestor Tree we find John M. Fine, 1818-1878; George W. Roberts, 1808-1880; and Thomas Collins, 1810-1880........A separate Outline Descendant Tree is shown for each of those names.

There are over 400 different family names included in the charts presented. Interesting stories are connected with many of the names.

Marland Estate officials are always glad to meet with Marland and other family relatives to share information. The citizens of Ponca City are proud of the Marland Estate. For information or if you wish to notify the Estate officials about your relationship with the Marland family relatives, please write to:

Director, THE MARLAND ESTATE
901 Monument Road
Ponca City, Oklahoma 74604

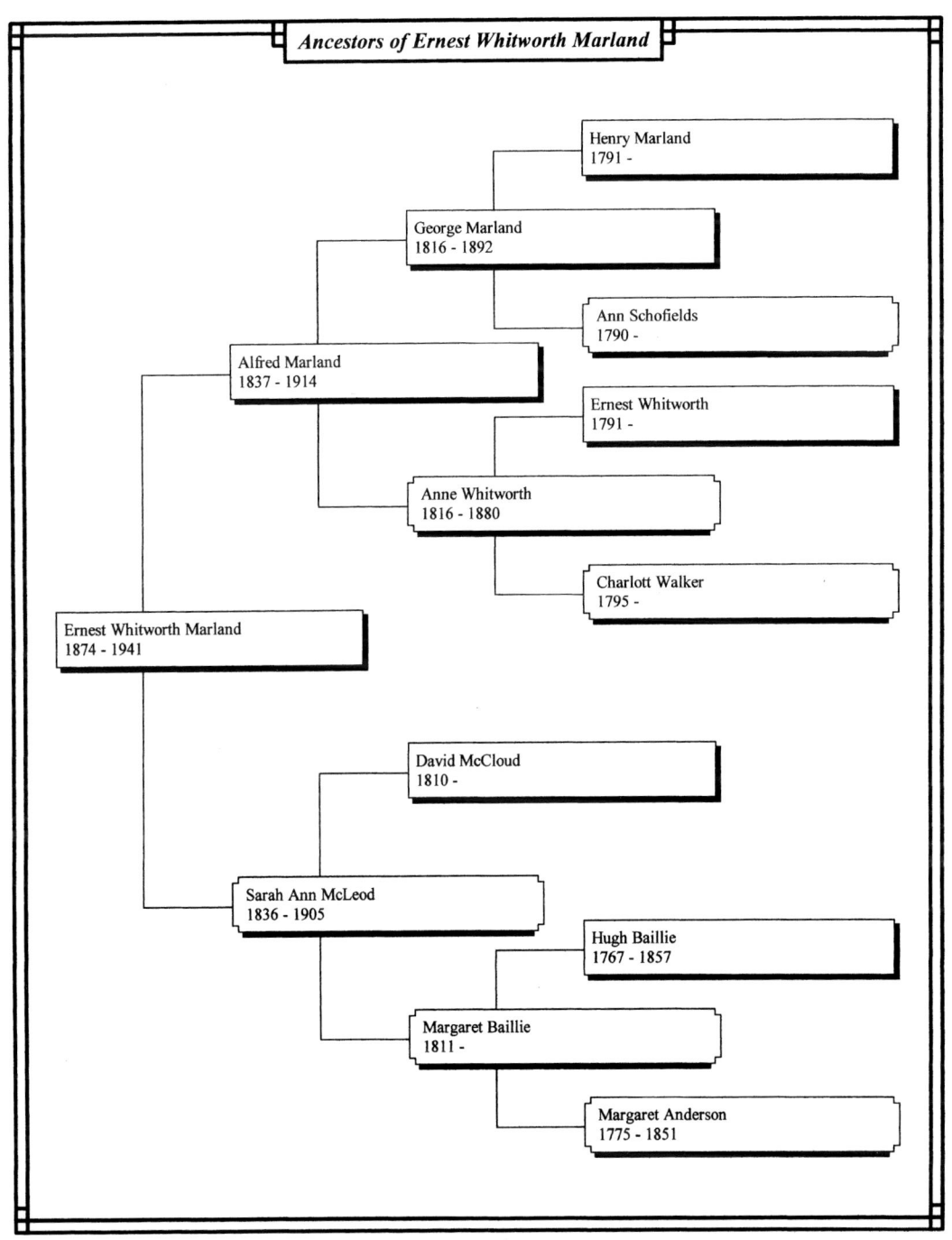

THE GENEALOGY OF THE MARLAND FAMILY

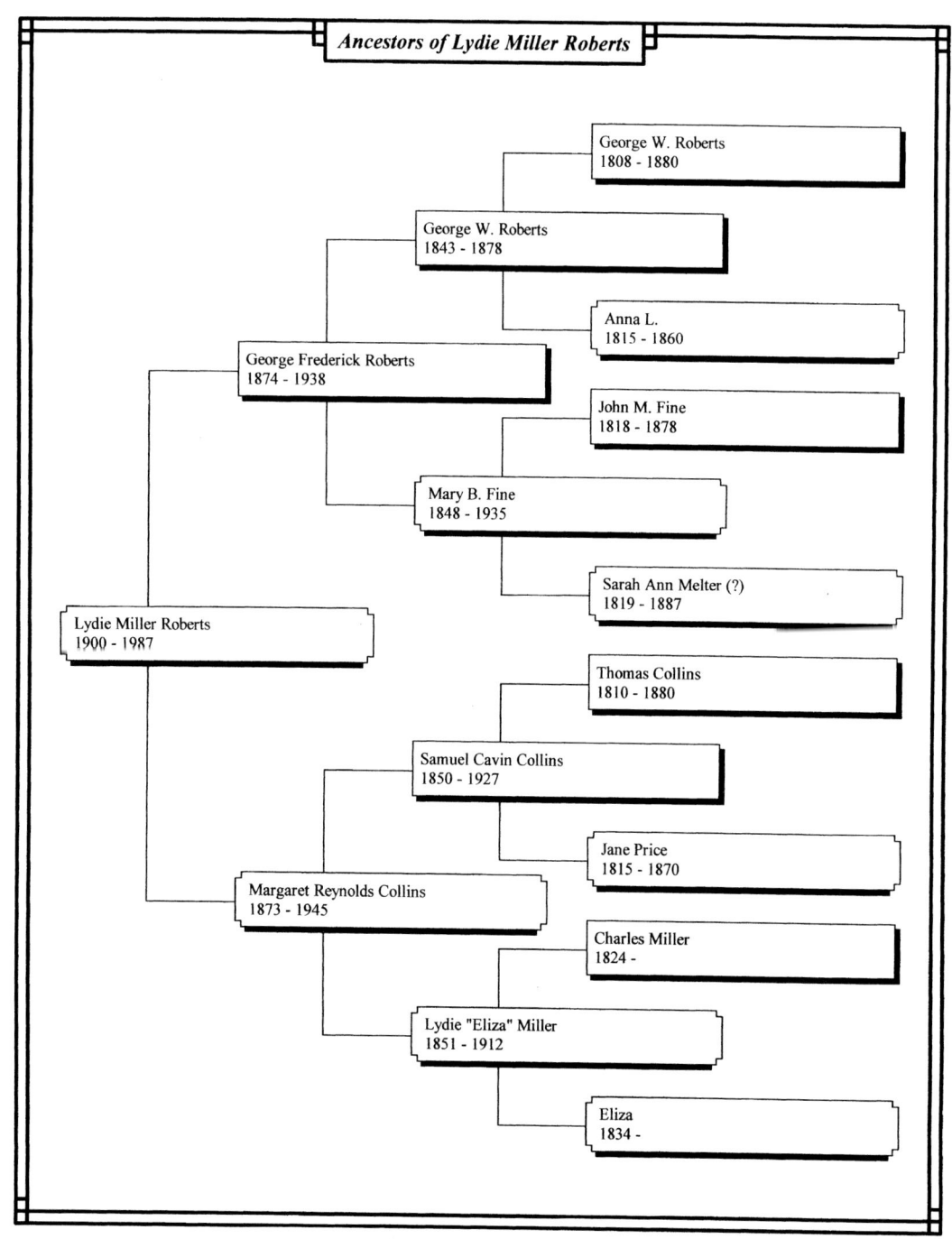

Descendants of George Marland

1 George Marland b: January 28, 1816 in Ashton-Under-Lyne, Lancashire, England d: January 08, 1892 in Pittsburgh, Allegheny County, Pennsylvania
. +Anne Whitworth b: 1816 in Lancashire, England d: Aft. 1880 in Pittsburgh, Allegheny County, Pennsylvania
.... 2 Alfred Marland b: March 02, 1837 in Ashton-Under-Lyne, Lancashire, England d: March 31, 1914 in Ponca City, Kay County, Oklahoma
.... +Sarah Ann McLeod b: October 12, 1836 in Dundee, Angus County, Scotland ? d: March 31, 1905 in Pittsburgh, Allegheny County, Pennsylvania
.... 3 Charlotte Anne (Lottie) Marland b: December 10, 1869 in Pittsburgh, Allegheny County, Pennsylvania d: July 11, 1927 in Ponca City, Kay County, Oklahoma
.... 3 Ignatia M. Marland b: November 04, 1871 in Pittsburgh, Allegheny County, Pennsylvania d: December 17, 1951 in New York City, New York
.... +Samuel W. Harper b: March 01, 1863 in Pittsburgh, Allegheny County, Pennsylvania d: Aft. 1920 in Pennsylvania
.... *2nd Husband of Ignatia M. Marland:
.... +Louis Kossuth Rittenhouse b: October 19, 1879 in New York City, New York d: October 28, 1924 in Orange, Essex County, New Jersey
.... 3 Ernest Whitworth Marland b: May 08, 1874 in Pittsburgh, Allegheny County, Pennsylvania d: October 03, 1941 in Ponca City, Kay County, Oklahoma
.... +Mary Virginia Collins b: July 07, 1876 in Philadelphia, Pennsylvania d: June 06, 1926 in Ponca City, Kay County, Oklahoma
.... *2nd Wife of Ernest Whitworth Marland:
.... +Lydie Miller Roberts b: April 07, 1900 in Philadelphia, Philadelphia, Pennsylvania d: July 27, 1987 in Ponca City, Kay County, Oklahoma
.... 3 Alfred Marland, Jr. b: January 1877 in Pittsburgh, Allegheny County, Pennsylvania d: July 19, 1877 in Pittsburgh, Allegheny County, Pennsylvania
.... 2 John Marland b: April 1839 in Ashton-under-Lyne, Lancashire, England
.... 2 Ratcliffe Marland b: March 1840 in Ashton-under-Lyne, Lancashire, England
.... 2 Henry Marland b: May 1841 in Ashton-under-Lyne, Lancashire, England d: July 16, 1934 in Wilmington, Delaware
.... +Elizabeth Fletcher b: May 1842 in England d: October 24, 1928 in Wilmington, Delaware
.... 3 Sarah Marland b: March 1865 in England d: 1950 in Wilmington, Delaware
.... +John Barnes b: June 1847 in England d: Bef. 1920
.... 4 Elizabeth Barnes b: May 1896 in New Jersey
.... 3 Ann Marland b: 1867 in England d: September 15, 1876 in Pittsburgh, Allegheny County, Pennsylvania
.... 3 Albert Marland b: December 1868 in England
.... 3 George Harry Marland b: March 17, 1872 in Pittsburgh, Allegheny County, Pennsylvania
.... 3 Lida Gehring Marland b: January 14, 1874 in Pittsburgh, Allegheny County, Pennsylvania d: September 14, 1954 in Wilmington, Delaware
.... +Schofield
.... 3 Mary Elizabeth Marland b: March 15, 1876 in Pittsburgh, Allegheny Co., PA
.... 3 Martha Marland b: October 31, 1880 in Pittsburgh, Allegheny County, Pennsylvania
.... 2 Mary Marland b: October 12, 1845 in Ashton-under-Lyne , Lancashire, England
.... 2 George Marland b: in Ashton-under-Lyne , Lancashire, England
.... +Hannah Turnock
.... 3 Alfred Marland b: 1873
.... 3 Jessie Marland

.... 2 Joel Marland b: April 23, 1853 in Ashton-under-Lyne , Lancashire, England d: March 04, 1911 in Cleveland, Cuyahoga County, Ohio
.... +Ann June Main b: February 1854 in England
.... 3 Lillie Marland b: December 1883 d: September 11, 1961
.... +X. Davis
.... *2nd Husband of Lillie Marland:
.... +Jim Carson d: 1960 in Cleveland, Cuyahoga County, Ohio
.... 3 William E. Marland b: June 1886 in Allegheny Co., PA (Stowe Twp.) d: March 1949
.... +Margaret b: 1887 in Pennsylvania
.... 4 William Marland b: 1924
.... *2nd Wife of William E. Marland:
.... +Fayette b: 1892 in Pennsylvania
.... 3 Alfred Marland b: January 1888 in Allegheny Co., Pennsylvania d: April 19, 1946 in Columbus, Franklin County, Ohio
.... +Alma Katherine Christine Nagle b: March 1892 in Allegheny Co., Pennsylvania d: August 12, 1942 in Columbus, Franklin County, Ohio
.... 4 Charles A. Marland b: January 09, 1912 in Columbus, Franklin County, Ohio d: December 15, 1975 in St. Petersburg, Pinellas Co., Florida
.... +Martha Green
.... *2nd Wife of Charles A. Marland:
.... +Unknown #1
.... 4 Edward J. Marland b: October 27, 1913 in Cleveland, Cuyahoga County, Ohio d: March 06, 1983 in Columbus, Franklin County, Ohio
.... +Bertha B. Schilling b: September 15, 1918 in Columbus, Franklin County, Ohio d: September 11, 2000 in Gahanna, Ohio
.... 4 Arthur William Marland b: January 08, 1916 in Columbus, Franklin County, Ohio d: May 25, 1993 in Ft. Myers Beach, Lee County, Florida
.... +Mary Florence Boggs b: July 30, 1914 in West Jefferson, Williams County ?, Ohio d: April 25, 2000 in Syracuse, Onandoga County, New York
.... 4 Hazel Marie Marland b: January 22, 1918 in Columbus, Franklin County, Ohio
.... +Harry McCabe
.... 4 Dorothy Marland b: Abt. 1921 d: in Hollywood, Florida
.... +X. Marcum
.... 4 Robert Ernest Marland b: March 16, 1926 in Columbus, Franklin County, Ohio d: February 24, 1997 in Columbus, Franklin County, Ohio
.... +Florence
.... 2 Charlott Ann Marland b: July 27, 1858 in Ashton-Under-Lyne , Lancashire, England
.... +Smith
.... 2 James Marland b: October 22, 1861 in Ashton-under-Lyne , Lancashire, England d: March 24, 1955 in Washington, Washington County, Pennsylvania
.... +Anna Eliza Sperring b: April 1867 in Birmingham, England d: May 13, 1934 in Washington, Washington County, Pennsylvania
.... 3 Ignatius Marland b: December 1888 in Beltzhoover, Allegheny County, Pennsylvania d: July 01, 1965
.... +Walter Baumiller,Sr b: January 19, 1888 d: March 25, 1956
.... 4 Lillian Lucilla Baumiller b: February 01, 1912 d: May 22, 1962 in Meadville, Pa
.... +Pistorius d: November 03, 1934
.... 4 James Albert Baumiller b: January 07, 1913 d: February 02, 1913

.... 4 Walter Baumiller,Jr b: March 11, 1914 d: January 29, 1979 in Pittsburgh, Allegheny County, Pennsylvania
.... 4 Charles Willard Baumiller b: November 09, 1916 d: February 1988 in Pittsburgh, Allegheny County, Pennsylvania
.... 4 Kenneth Mirle Baumiller b: September 16, 1919 d: June 1983 in Venetia, Pennsylvania
.... 4 Richard Baumiller b: October 10, 1923 d: April 25, 1990 in ?
.... 4 Blanch Marland Baumiller b: November 13, 1924 d: February 13, 1927
.... 4 Gearldine Baumiller b: July 06, 1927
.... 4 Ethyl Myral Baumiller b: February 14, 1932 d: February 26, 1932
.... 3 Albert Marland b: June 22, 1890 in Beltzhoover, Allegheny County, Pennsylvania d: March 1966 in Washinton, Washington County, Pennsylvania
.... 3 Blanche Marland b: August 11, 1891 in Beltzhoover, Allegheny County, Pennsylvania d: February 29, 1964 in Washington, Washington County, Pennsylvania
.... 3 Mary Virginia Marland b: November 16, 1903 in Washington County, Pennsylvania d: February 12, 1978 in Washington, Washington County, Pennsylvania
.... +Charles Driehorst Myers b: 1903 in Washington, Washington County, Pennsylvania d: May 30, 1955 in Oil City, Venango County, Pennsylvania
.... 4 Matilda Anne Myers b: August 28, 1925 in Washington, Washington County, Pennsylvania
.... 4 Richard Marland Myers b: December 29, 1931 in Bradford, McKean County, Pennsylvania
.... +Wilma Virginia Winters b: October 06, 1937 in Washington , Washington County, Pennsylvania

DESCENDANTS OF GEORGE ROBERTS

1 George W. Roberts b: 1808 in Pennsylvania d: Bef. 1880 in Philadelphia, PA
. +Anna L. b: 1815 in Pennsylvania d: Bef. 1860 in Philadelphia, PA
.... 2 Rachael W. Roberts b: 1835 in Philadelphia, PA
.... 2 Anna L. Roberts b: 1841 in Philadelphia, PA
.... 2 George W. Roberts b: 1843 in Philadelphia, PA-West Side d: Abt. 1878 in Philadelphia, PA
.... +Mary B. Fine b: June 28, 1848 in New Jersey d: November 23, 1935 in Ambler, Montgomery Co., Pennsylvania
.... 3 Kate Crittendon Roberts b: April 26, 1867 in Philadelphia, Pennsylvania d: May 10, 1913 in Philadelphia, PA
.... +John James Hare b: October 20, 1865 in Philadelphia, Pennsylvania d: April 19, 1918 in Philadelphia, PA
.... 4 Alice W. Hare b: September 1898 in Philadelphia, PA d: September 01, 1928 in Philadelphia, Philadelphia Co., Pennsylvania
.... 4 Katherine Hare b: September 05, 1902 in Philadelphia, Pennsylvania d: January 1971 in Erie, Erie County, Pennsylvania
.... +Harold F. Roling b: June 21, 1904 in Pennsylvania d: May 13, 1968 in Hatboro, Montgomery County, PA
.... 5 Jay Roling b: May 14, 1938
.... *2nd Husband of Katherine Hare:
.... +Marcus (Mark) Waldo b: December 30, 1906 in Erie, Erie County, Pennsylvania d: December 14, 1993 in Meadville, Pennsylvania
.... 4 Marie Amory Hare b: December 29, 1905 in Philadelphia, PA d: September 30, 1975 in Flourtown, Montgomery Co., PA
.... +Frederick William Young b: 1890 in Pennsylvania d: December 25, 1955 in Flourtown, Montgomery County, Pennsylvania
.... 3 George Frederick Roberts b: January 17, 1874 in Philadelphia, Philadelphia County, Pennsylvania d: June 24, 1938 in Flourtown, Montgomery County, Pennsylvania
.... +Margaret Reynolds Collins b: June 09, 1873 in Philadelphia, Philadelphia County, Pennsylvania d: December 19, 1945 in Philadelphia, Philadelphia County, Pennsylvania
.... 4 George Roberts (Marland) b: November 19, 1897 in Philadelphia, Pennsylvania d: January 19, 1957 in Tulsa, Tulsa Co., Oklahoma
.... +LaVerne Ann Donahue b: September 05, 1907 in Ponca City, Kay County, Oklahoma d: August 04, 1973 in Tulsa, Tulsa County, Oklahoma
.... 5 Margaret (Margo) Whitworth Marland b: November 09, 1930 in Ponca City, Kay County, Oklahoma d: February 15, 1977 in Dallas, Texas
.... +James Murray Henry, Jr. b: 1926
.... 6 Ann Roberts Henry b: 1957 in Tulsa, Tulsa County, Oklahoma
.... 6 Margaret Marland Henry b: 1961 in Tulsa, Tulsa County, Oklahoma
.... 4 Lydie Miller Roberts b: April 07, 1900 in Philadelphia, Philadelphia, Pennsylvania d: July 27, 1987 in Ponca City, Kay County, Oklahoma
.... +Ernest Whitworth Marland b: May 08, 1874 in Pittsburgh, Allegheny County, Pennsylvania d: October 03, 1941 in Ponca City, Kay County, Oklahoma
.... 4 Ernest Marland Roberts b: April 27, 1904 in Philadelphia, Pennsylvania d: August 11, 1991 in Edmonds, Snohomish County, Washington
.... +Virginia B. Seton b: October 12, 1907 in New Jersey d: October 12, 1982 in Doylestown, Bucks County, Pennsylvania
.... 5 Marland Seton (Bill) Roberts b: April 28, 1929 in Ponca City, Kay County, Oklahoma

.... +Joan Lorraine Carsley b: August 06, 1934 in Bryn Mawr, Delaware County, Pennsylvania
.... 6 William Marland Roberts b: September 16, 1952 in Fort Smith Virginia d: November 17, 1979 in Seattle, King County, Washington
.... 6 Michael Ernest Roberts b: September 07, 1953 in Norfolk, Virginia
.... +Sandy Love
.... 6 Deborah Roberts b: May 10, 1956 in Philadelphia, Philadelphia, Pennsylvania
.... +David Hills
.... *2nd Husband of Deborah Roberts:
.... +Jerry Hamilton
.... 6 Penny Roberts b: September 29, 1960 in Federal Way, King County, Washington
.... +Vern Geyman
.... *2nd Husband of Penny Roberts:
.... +Terry Wallace
.... 5 Donald Roberts b: October 31, 1931 in Flourtown, Montgomery County, Pennsylvania d: May 2000 in Philadelphia, Philadelphia Co., Pennsylvania
.... +Francis d: in Philadelphia, Philadelphia Co., Pennsylvania
.... 6 Mark Roberts
.... 6 David Roberts
.... *2nd Wife of Ernest Marland Roberts:
.... +Virginia Prediger b: October 12, 1907 in Montgomery County, Pennsylvania
.... 5 Dru Roberts b: 1943
.... *3rd Wife of Ernest Marland Roberts:
.... +Verna Bosse b: March 08, 1914
.... 4 Virginia Roberts b: July 03, 1909 in Philadelphia, Pennsylvania d: August 03, 1981 in Dunedin, Pinellas County, Florida
.... +LeRoy Jacob Hersh b: October 12, 1900 in Trenton, New Jersey d: November 20, 1960 in Omaha, Sarpy County, Nebraska
.... 5 Jack Hersh
.... 5 Jill Hersh d: Bef. 2004
.... 5 Dennis E. Hersh
*2nd Wife of George W. Roberts:
. +Isabella b: 1818 in Pennsylvania
.... 2 Susan Roberts b: 1853

DESCENDANTS OF DAVID MCCLOUD

1 David McCloud b: Abt. 1810 in Scotland
. +Margaret Baillie b: May 1811 in Dundee, Angus County, Scotland
.... 2 Sarah Ann McLeod b: October 12, 1836 in Dundee, Angus County, Scotland ? d: March 31, 1905 in Pittsburgh, Allegheny County, Pennsylvania
.... +Henry Smith b: 1831 in Ferry Hill, Durham County, England d: Abt. 1867 in Pittsburgh, Allegheny County, Pennsylvania
.... 3 Sarah Anne Smith b: December 12, 1856 in Middlesboro, York County, England d: March 13, 1931 in Los Angeles, California
.... +John P. Kenney b: April 1849 in Allegheny City, Allegheny Co., Pennsylvania d: October 27, 1901 in Wadestown, Mononglia County, West Virginia
.... 3 David Henry Smith b: September 27, 1858 in Middlesbrough, York County, England d: March 09, 1915 in Pittsburgh, Allegheny County, Pennsylvania
.... +Elizabeth Grace Zehfuss b: August 1859 in Pittsburg, Allegheny County, Pennsylvania d: April 14, 1935 in Pittsburgh, Allegheny County, Pennsylvania
.... 3 Jane Elizabeth (Mary) Smith b: September 27, 1858 in Middlesboro, York County, England d: December 20, 1899 in Pittsburgh, Allegheny County, Pennsylvania
.... +Abraham G. Croner b: January 1852 in Pittsburg, Pennsylvania d: January 06, 1917 in Los Angeles, California
.... 3 Margaret Jane Smith b: February 25, 1862 in Middlesboro, York County, England d: October 15, 1938 in Los Angeles, California
.... +Andrew K. Martell b: March 21, 1853 in New York , d: July 10, 1929 in Los Angeles, California
.... 3 William John Baily Smith b: August 20, 1865 in Pittsburg, Allegheny County, Pennsylvania
.... +Agnes E. Dilworth b: October 20, 1872 in Pittsburgh, Allegheny County, Pennsylvania
.... *2nd Husband of Sarah Ann McLeod:
.... +Alfred Marland b: March 02, 1837 in Ashton-Under-Lyne, Lancashire, England d: March 31, 1914 in Ponca City, Kay County, Oklahoma
.... 3 Charlotte Anne (Lottie) Marland b: December 10, 1869 in Pittsburgh, Allegheny County, Pennsylvania d: July 11, 1927 in Ponca City, Kay County, Oklahoma
.... 3 Ignatia M. Marland b: November 04, 1871 in Pittsburgh, Allegheny County, Pennsylvania d: December 17, 1951 in New York City, New York
.... +Samuel W. Harper b: March 01, 1863 in Pittsburgh, Allegheny County, Pennsylvania d: Aft. 1920 in Pennsylvania
.... *2nd Husband of Ignatia M. Marland:
.... +Louis Kossuth Rittenhouse b: October 19, 1879 in New York City, New York d: October 28, 1924 in Orange, Essex County, New Jersey
.... 3 Ernest Whitworth Marland b: May 08, 1874 in Pittsburgh, Allegheny County, Pennsylvania d: October 03, 1941 in Ponca City, Kay County, Oklahoma
.... +Mary Virginia Collins b: July 07, 1876 in Philadelphia, Pennsylvania d: June 06, 1926 in Ponca City, Kay County, Oklahoma
.... *2nd Wife of Ernest Whitworth Marland:
.... +Lydie Miller Roberts b: April 07, 1900 in Philadelphia, Philadelphia, Pennsylvania d: July 27, 1987 in Ponca City, Kay County, Oklahoma
.... 3 Alfred Marland, Jr. b: January 1877 in Pittsburgh, Allegheny County, Pennsylvania d: July 19, 1877 in Pittsburgh, Allegheny County, Pennsylvania
.... 2 Mary Ann McLeod b: 1838 in Dundee, Angus Co., Scotland
.... +John Young

.... 2 John Baillie McCloud b: 1840 in Scotland d: February 10, 1883 in Pittsburgh, Allegheny County, Pennsylvania
.... +Ann Young b: March 10, 1836 in Saint Vigeans, Angus County, Scotland d: January 24, 1896 in Patterson, Passaic County, New Jersey
.... 3 Elizabeth McCloud b: 1868 in Dundee, Angus Co., Scotland
.... +David Johnstone
.... 3 Philip McCloud b: April 07, 1872 in Pittsburgh, Allegheny County, Pennsylvania d: September 06, 1944 in Paterson, New Jersey
.... +Joan Watson Smith d: January 01, 1959 in Paterson, New Jersey
.... 3 David McCloud b: April 01, 1874 in Pittsburgh, Allegheny County, Pennsylvania
.... +Jessie Robertson
.... *2nd Wife of David McCloud:
.... +Elizabeth Johnstone
.... 3 Margaret McCloud b: 1876 in Pittsburgh, Allegheny County, Pennsylvania
.... +Joseph Buckley

DESCENDANTS OF THOMAS COLLINS

1 Thomas Collins b: 1810 in Ireland d: Bef. 1880 in Philadelphia, Pennsylvania
. +Jane Price b: 1815 in Maryland d: Bef. 1870 in Philadelphia, Pennsylvania
.... 2 William Collins b: 1837 in Philadelphia, PA
.... +Ellen b: 1837 in Delaware Co., Pennsylvania
.... 3 Jane Collins b: 1862 in Philadelphia, PA
.... 3 William Collins b: 1867 in Philadelphia, PA
.... 3 Mary Collins b: 1869 in Philadelphia, PA
.... 3 Ellen Collins b: 1872 in Philadelphia, PA
.... 3 Robert Collins b: 1875 in Philadelphia, PA
.... 2 Nicholas Collins b: 1844 in Philadelphia, Pennsylvania
.... +Mary Carey b: 1849
.... 3 John M. Collins b: 1873
.... 3 Mary Collins b: 1878
.... 2 Mary Collins b: 1848 in Philadelphia, Pennsylvania
.... 2 Samuel Cavin Collins b: July 22, 1850 in Philadelphia, Pennsylvania d: February 25, 1927 in Ponca City, Kay County, Oklahoma
.... +Lydie "Eliza" Miller b: March 09, 1851 in Philadelphia, Pennsylvania d: August 02, 1912 in Philadelphia, Pennsylvania
.... 3 Margaret Reynolds Collins b: June 09, 1873 in Philadelphia, Philadelphia County, Pennsylvania d: December 19, 1945 in Philadelphia, Philadelphia County, Pennsylvania
.... +George Frederick Roberts b: January 17, 1874 in Philadelphia, Philadelphia County, Pennsylvania d: June 24, 1938 in Flourtown, Montgomery County, Pennsylvania
.... 4 George Roberts (Marland) b: November 19, 1897 in Philadelphia, Pennsylvania d: January 19, 1957 in Tulsa, Tulsa Co., Oklahoma
.... +LaVerne Ann Donahue b: September 05, 1907 in Ponca City, Kay County, Oklahoma d: August 04, 1973 in Tulsa, Tulsa County, Oklahoma
.... 5 Margaret (Margo) Whitworth Marland b: November 09, 1930 in Ponca City, Kay County, Oklahoma d: February 15, 1977 in Dallas, Texas
.... +James Murray Henry, Jr. b: 1926
.... 6 Ann Roberts Henry b: 1957 in Tulsa, Tulsa County, Oklahoma
.... 6 Margaret Marland Henry b: 1961 in Tulsa, Tulsa County, Oklahoma
.... 4 Lydie Miller Roberts b: April 07, 1900 in Philadelphia, Philadelphia, Pennsylvania d: July 27, 1987 in Ponca City, Kay County, Oklahoma
.... +[1] Ernest Whitworth Marland b: May 08, 1874 in Pittsburgh, Allegheny County, Pennsylvania d: October 03, 1941 in Ponca City, Kay County, Oklahoma
.... 4 Ernest Marland Roberts b: April 27, 1904 in Philadelphia, Pennsylvania d: August 11, 1991 in Edmonds, Snohomish County, Washington
.... +Virginia B. Seton b: October 12, 1907 in New Jersey d: October 12, 1982 in Doylestown, Bucks County, Pennsylvania
.... 5 Marland Seton (Bill) Roberts b: April 28, 1929 in Ponca City, Kay County, Oklahoma
.... +Joan Lorraine Carsley b: August 06, 1934 in Bryn Mawr, Delaware County, Pennsylvania
.... 6 William Marland Roberts b: September 16, 1952 in Fort Smith Virginia d: November 17, 1979 in Seattle, King County, Washington
.... 6 Michael Ernest Roberts b: September 07, 1953 in Norfolk, Virginia
.... +Sandy Love

.... 6 Deborah Roberts b: May 10, 1956 in Philadelphia, Philadelphia,
             Pennsylvania
.... +David Hills
.... *2nd Husband of Deborah Roberts:
.... +Jerry Hamilton
.... 6 Penny Roberts b: September 29, 1960 in Federal Way, King County,
             Washington
.... +Vern Geyman
.... *2nd Husband of Penny Roberts:
.... +Terry Wallace
.... 5 Donald Roberts b: October 31, 1931 in Flourtown, Montgomery County,
          Pennsylvania d: May 2000 in Philadelphia, Philadelphia Co., Pennsylvania
.... +Francis d: in Philadelphia, Philadelphia Co., Pennsylvania
.... 6 Mark Roberts
.... 6 David Roberts
...... *2nd Wife of Ernest Marland Roberts:
...... +Virginia Prediger b: October 12, 1907 in Montgomery County, Pennsylvania
.... 5 Dru Roberts b: 1943
...... *3rd Wife of Ernest Marland Roberts:
...... +Verna Bosse b: March 08, 1914
...... 4 Virginia Roberts b: July 03, 1909 in Philadelphia, Pennsylvania d: August 03, 1981
       in Dunedin, Pinellas County, Florida
.... +LeRoy Jacob Hersh b: October 12, 1900 in Trenton, New Jersey d: November 20
          1960 in Omaha, Sarpy County, Nebraska
.... 5 Jack Hersh
.... 5 Jill Hersh d: Bef. 2004
.... 5 Dennis E. Hersh
.. 3 Mary Virginia Collins b: July 07, 1876 in Philadelphia, Pennsylvania d: June 06, 1926 in
    Ponca City, Kay County, Oklahoma
...... +[1] Ernest Whitworth Marland b: May 08, 1874 in Pittsburgh, Allegheny County,
       Pennsylvania d: October 03, 1941 in Ponca City, Kay County, Oklahoma
.. 3 Nellie G. Collins b: June 09, 1881 in Philadelphia, Pennsylvania d: Bef. 1957 in
    Pennsylvania
...... +Frank J. Plummer b: April 25, 1881 in Boston, Massachusetts
.... 4 Samuel C. Plummer b: Abt. 1904 in Philadelphia, Philadelphia, Pennsylvania
.... 4 Frank J. Plummer, Jr. b: Abt. 1908 in Philadelphia, Philadelphia, Pennsylvania
. 3 Samuel Cavin Collins,Jr. b: October 10, 1883 in Philadelphia, Pennsylvania d: January
   02, 1957 in Ponca City, Kay County, Oklahoma
...... +Florence Weisenberger b: March 30, 1890 in Philadelphia,Philadelphia Pennsylvania d:
       November 04, 1977 in Ponca City, Kay County, Oklahoma
.... 4 Lydie Virginia Collins b: April 09, 1918 in Ponca City, Kay County, Oklahoma d:
          June 1986 in Roswell, New Mexico
.... +Rexell V. Desmond b: October 01, 1915 in Oklahoma d: July 12, 1998 in Roswell
             New Mexico
.... 5 Cavin Desmond b: August 16, 1946 d: May 27, 1998 in New Mexico
.... 4 Florence Ann Collins b: 1921 in Ponca City, Kay County, Oklahoma
.... +Gordon E. Holland
.... 5 Jack Holland

.... 3 Bessie G. Collins b: April 02, 1887 in Philadelphia, Pennsylvania d: Abt. 1959 in Philadelphia, Pennsylvania
.... +Edward B. Webster b: December 12, 1886 in Philadelphia, Pennsylvania
.... *2nd Husband of Bessie G. Collins:
.... +Clarence E. Olden b: 1884 in New Jersey
.... *3rd Husband of Bessie G. Collins:
.... +Bernard Lupin b: 1889 in Philadelphia, PA
.... *2nd Wife of Samuel Cavin Collins:
.... +Clara Malinda Kaseman b: January 18, 1869 in Shamokin, Northumberland Co., Pennsylvania d: April 03, 1939 in Ponca City, Kay County, Oklahoma
.... 2 Ellen Collins b: 1854 in Philadelphia, Pennsylvania
.... 2 Sallie Collins b: 1858 in Philadelphia, Pennsylvania

DESCENDANTS OF JOHN FINE

1 John M. Fine b: 1818 in New Jersey d: May 17, 1878 in Philadelphia, Pennsylvania
. +Sarah Ann Melter (?) b: 1819 in New Jersey d: July 21, 1887 in Philadelphia, Pennsylvania
.... 2 Albert H. Fine b: 1840 in New Jersey d: July 14, 1889 in Philadelphia, Pennsylvania
.... 2 Ann E. Fine b: 1841 d: August 25, 1865
.... 2 Martha Fine b: 1843
.... 2 William M. Fine b: 1844
.... 2 Mary B. Fine b: June 28, 1848 in New Jersey d: November 23, 1935 in Ambler, Montgomery Co., Pennsylvania
.... +George W. Roberts b: 1843 in Philadelphia, PA-West Side d: Abt. 1878 in Philadelphia, PA
.... 3 Kate Crittendon Roberts b: April 26, 1867 in Philadelphia, Pennsylvania d: May 10, 1913 in Philadelphia, PA
.... +John James Hare b: October 20, 1865 in Philadelphia, Pennsylvania d: April 19, 1918 in Philadelphia, PA
.... 4 Alice W. Hare b: September 1898 in Philadelphia, PA d: September 01, 1928 in Philadelphia, Philadelphia Co., Pennsylvania
.... 4 Katherine Hare b: September 05, 1902 in Philadelphia, Pennsylvania d: January 1971 in Erie, Erie County, Pennsylvania
.... +Harold F. Roling b: June 21, 1904 in Pennsylvania d: May 13, 1968 in Hatboro, Montgomery County, PA
.... 5 Jay Roling b: May 14, 1938
.... *2nd Husband of Katherine Hare:
.... +Marcus (Mark) Waldo b: December 30, 1906 in Erie, Erie County, Pennsylvania d: December 14, 1993 in Meadville, Pennsylvania
.... 4 Marie Amory Hare b: December 29, 1905 in Philadelphia, PA d: September 30, 1975 in Flourtown, Montgomery Co., PA
.... +Frederick William Young b: 1890 in Pennsylvania d: December 25, 1955 in Flourtown, Montgomery County, Pennsylvania
.... 3 George Frederick Roberts b: January 17, 1874 in Philadelphia, Philadelphia County, Pennsylvania d: June 24, 1938 in Flourtown, Montgomery County, Pennsylvania
.... +Margaret Reynolds Collins b: June 09, 1873 in Philadelphia, Philadelphia County, Pennsylvania d: December 19, 1945 in Philadelphia, Philadelphia County, Pennsylvania
.... 4 George Roberts (Marland) b: November 19, 1897 in Philadelphia, Pennsylvania d: January 19, 1957 in Tulsa, Tulsa Co., Oklahoma
.... +LaVerne Ann Donahue b: September 05, 1907 in Ponca City, Kay County, Oklahoma d: August 04, 1973 in Tulsa, Tulsa County, Oklahoma
.... 5 Margaret (Margo) Whitworth Marland b: November 09, 1930 in Ponca City, Kay County, Oklahoma d: February 15, 1977 in Dallas, Texas
.... +James Murray Henry, Jr. b: 1926
.... 6 Ann Roberts Henry b: 1957 in Tulsa, Tulsa County, Oklahoma
.... 6 Margaret Marland Henry b: 1961 in Tulsa, Tulsa County, Oklahoma
.... 4 Lydie Miller Roberts b: April 07, 1900 in Philadelphia, Philadelphia, Pennsylvania d: July 27, 1987 in Ponca City, Kay County, Oklahoma
.... +Ernest Whitworth Marland b: May 08, 1874 in Pittsburgh, Allegheny County, Pennsylvania d: October 03, 1941 in Ponca City, Kay County, Oklahoma
.... 4 Ernest Marland Roberts b: April 27, 1904 in Philadelphia, Pennsylvania d: August 11, 1991 in Edmonds, Snohomish County, Washington
.... +Virginia B. Seton b: October 12, 1907 in New Jersey d: October 12, 1982 in Doylestown, Bucks County, Pennsylvania

```
............     5 Marland Seton (Bill) Roberts  b: April 28, 1929 in Ponca City, Kay County,
                    Oklahoma
............     +Joan Lorraine Carsley  b: August 06, 1934 in Bryn Mawr, Delaware County,
                    Pennsylvania
............        6 William Marland Roberts  b: September 16, 1952 in Fort Smith
                        Virginia  d: November 17, 1979 in Seattle, King County, Washington
............        6 Michael Ernest Roberts  b: September 07, 1953 in Norfolk, Virginia
............        +Sandy Love
............        6 Deborah Roberts  b: May 10, 1956 in Philadelphia, Philadelphia,
                        Pennsylvania
............        +David Hills
............        *2nd Husband of Deborah Roberts:
............        +Jerry Hamilton
............        6 Penny Roberts  b: September 29, 1960 in Federal Way, King County,
                        Washington
............        +Vern Geyman
............        *2nd Husband of Penny Roberts:
............        +Terry Wallace
............     5 Donald Roberts  b: October 31, 1931 in Flourtown, Montgomery County,
                    Pennsylvania  d: May 2000 in Philadelphia, Philadelphia Co., Pennsylvania
............     +Francis  d: in Philadelphia, Philadelphia Co., Pennsylvania
............        6 Mark Roberts
............        6 David Roberts
............  *2nd Wife of Ernest Marland Roberts:
............     +Virginia Prediger  b: October 12, 1907 in Montgomery County, Pennsylvania
............     5 Dru Roberts  b: 1943
............  *3rd Wife of Ernest Marland Roberts:
............     +Verna Bosse  b: March 08, 1914
............  4 Virginia Roberts  b: July 03, 1909 in Philadelphia, Pennsylvania  d: August 03, 1981
                 in Dunedin, Pinellas County, Florida
............  +LeRoy Jacob Hersh  b: October 12, 1900 in Trenton, New Jersey  d: November 20,
                 1960 in Omaha, Sarpy County, Nebraska
............     5 Jack Hersh
............     5 Jill Hersh  d: Bef. 2004
............     5 Dennis E. Hersh
...  *2nd Husband of Mary B. Fine:
.......  +George Christian Fine  b: September 1860 in Cayuga County, New York  d: January 19,
            1954 in Montgomery Co., PA
...  2 George W. Fine  b: 1851 in New Jersey
...  2 John L. Fine  b: 1853 in New Jersey  d: July 07, 1901 in Philadelphia, Pennsylvania
...  2 Lewis S. Fine  b: 1855 in New Jersey
```

DESCENDANTS OF SARAH MCLEOD

1 Sarah Ann McLeod b: October 12, 1836 in Dundee, Angus County, Scotland ? d: March 31, 1905 in Pittsburgh, Allegheny County, Pennsylvania
. +Henry Smith b: 1831 in Ferry Hill, Durham County, England d: Abt. 1867 in Pittsburgh, Allegheny County, Pennsylvania
.... 2 Sarah Anne Smith b: December 12, 1856 in Middlesboro, York County, England d: March 13, 1931 in Los Angeles, California
.... +John P. Kenney b: April 1849 in Allegheny City, Allegheny Co., Pennsylvania d: October 27, 1901 in Wadestown, Mononglia County, West Virginia
.... 3 Franklin Rockefeller Kenney b: June 13, 1878 in Pittsburgh, Allegheny County, Pennsylvania d: November 25, 1954 in Los Angeles, Los Angeles County, California
.... +Nellie Torrence b: August 02, 1880 in Pittsburg, Allegheny County, Pennsylvania d: November 18, 1950 in Los Angeles, Los Angeles County, California
.... 4 William John Kenney b: June 16, 1904 in Oklahoma City, Oklahoma d: January 16, 1992 in Washington, D.C.
.... +Elinor Merill Craig b: February 15, 1909 d: June 03, 1991 in Washington, DC
.... 5 Elinor Merrill Kenney b: February 07, 1933 in San Francisco, California
.... +Philip Bransfield Brown d: January 02, 1980 in Washington, DC
.... *2nd Husband of Elinor Merrill Kenney:
.... +Norman Farquhar b: May 10, 1921 in Maryland d: July 14, 1992 in Washington, DC
.... 5 Priscilla Kenney b: October 03, 1936 in Washington, DC
.... +Edward James Streator
.... 5 David Torrance Kenney b: June 27, 1939 in Los Angeles, California
.... +Helen Bowen
.... 5 John Franklin Kenney b: 1940
.... 2 David Henry Smith b: September 27, 1858 in Middlesbrough, York County, England d: March 09, 1915 in Pittsburgh, Allegheny County, Pennsylvania
.... +Elizabeth Grace Zehfuss b: August 1859 in Pittsburg, Allegheny County, Pennsylvania d: April 14, 1935 in Pittsburgh, Allegheny County, Pennsylvania
.... 3 Annie Belle Smith b: November 1878 in Pittsburgh, Allegheny County, Pennsylvania
.... +Rudolf (Max) Rosenkranz b: 1873 in Germany
.... 4 Randolph Rosenkranz b: 1897 in Pittsburgh, Allegheny County, Pennsylvania
.... 3 George Thomas Smith b: January 1881 in Pittsburgh, Allegheny County, Pennsylvania d: February 10, 1957 in Pittsburgh, Allegheny County, Pennsylvania
.... +Lillie Mae b: 1883 in Pennsylvania d: May 02, 1951 in Pittsburgh, Allegheny County, Pennsylvania
.... 4 Albert Edward Smith b: January 27, 1901 in Pittsburg, Allegheny County, Pennsylvania
.... 4 Grace Elizabeth Smith b: July 22, 1906 in Pittsburgh, Allegheny County, Pennsylvania d: October 24, 1984 in Pittsburgh, Allegheny County, Pennsylvania
.... +Ralph H. Jones d: December 24, 1960 in Pittsburgh, Allegheny County, Pennsylvania
.... *2nd Husband of Grace Elizabeth Smith:
.... +Oscar M. Voelker b: April 28, 1900 in Pennsylvania d: June 14, 1976 in Pittsburgh, Allegheny County, Pennsylvania
.... 4 David H. Smith b: 1914 in Pittsburg, Allegheny County, Pennsylvania
.... 3 Lillie May Smith b: July 07, 1883 in Pittsburgh, Allegheny County, Pennsylvania
.... +William O. Jarvis b: July 03, 1880 in Pennsylvania

.... 4 Elizabeth Jarvis b: 1903
.... 4 William Oliver Jarvis b: 1907
.... 2 Jane Elizabeth (Mary) Smith b: September 27, 1858 in Middlesboro, York County, England d: December 20, 1899 in Pittsburgh, Allegheny County, Pennsylvania
.... +Abraham G. Croner b: January 1852 in Pittsburg, Pennsylvania d: January 06, 1917 in Los Angeles, California
.... 3 Edna Brown Croner b: July 01, 1880 in Pittsburgh, Allegheny County, Pennsylvania d: March 26, 1974 in Los Angeles, California
.... +Escaveille M. Davis b: 1879 in Maryland
.... *2nd Husband of Edna Brown Croner:
.... +Louis O. Schellenberger b: February 04, 1882 in Georgia d: March 16, 1945 in Los Angeles, California
.... 3 Charles Brokaw Croner b: March 04, 1882 in Pittsburgh, Allegheny County, Pennsylvania d: January 09, 1924 in Salt Lake City, Salt Lake County, Utah,
.... +Agnes Isabelle Buisseret b: May 27, 1886 in California d: December 02, 1975 in Hospital, Huntington Beach, Orange County, CA
.... 2 Margaret Jane Smith b: February 25, 1862 in Middlesboro, York County, England d: October 15, 1938 in Los Angeles, California
.... +Andrew K. Martell b: March 21, 1853 in New York , d: July 10, 1929 in Los Angeles, California
.... 3 Alberta Martell b: October 13, 1881 in Pittsburgh, Allegheny Co., PA
.... 3 Lillian Martell b: July 18, 1883 in Pittsburg,Allegheny County, Pennsylvania
.... +Charles J. Huber b: October 14, 1886 in Missouri d: September 18, 1966 in Los Angeles, California
.... *2nd Husband of Lillian Martell:
.... +Albert Milton Wells b: April 17, 1886 in Illinois d: December 21, 1969 in Los Angeles, California
.... 3 Marie Dorion Martell b: October 13, 1887 in Pittsburg, Pennsylvania d: January 10, 1946 in Alameda, Alameda County, California
.... +Edward William Buffington b: April 10, 1888 in Los Angeles. Los Angeles County, California d: December 03, 1947 in San Francisco, California
.... *2nd Husband of Marie Dorion Martell:
.... +Gordon Glen Glasgow b: July 14, 1898 in Illinois d: March 06, 1956 in San Francisco, California
.... 3 Margaret Jane Martell b: August 01, 1900 in Pittsburgh, Allegheny County, Pennsylvania d: September 21, 1944 in Los Angeles, Los Angeles County, California
.... +John (Jack) Adolph Herwig b: March 29, 1903 in Los Angeles, California d: November 13, 1976 in Brownsville, Cameron County, Texas
.... 4 Margaret J. Herwig b: 1926 in Los Angeles , California
.... 2 William John Baily Smith b: August 20, 1865 in Pittsburg, Allegheny County, Pennsylvania
.... +Agnes E. Dilworth b: October 20, 1872 in Pittsburgh, Allegheny County, Pennsylvania
*2nd Husband of Sarah Ann McLeod:
. +Alfred Marland b: March 02, 1837 in Ashton-Under-Lyne, Lancashire, England d: March 31, 1914 in Ponca City, Kay County, Oklahoma
.... 2 Charlotte Anne (Lottie) Marland b: December 10, 1869 in Pittsburgh, Allegheny County, Pennsylvania d: July 11, 1927 in Ponca City, Kay County, Oklahoma
.... 2 Ignatia M. Marland b: November 04, 1871 in Pittsburgh, Allegheny County, Pennsylvania d: December 17, 1951 in New York City, New York

.... +Samuel W. Harper b: March 01, 1863 in Pittsburgh, Allegheny County, Pennsylvania d: Aft. 1920 in Pennsylvania
.... *2nd Husband of Ignatia M. Marland:
.... +Louis Kossuth Rittenhouse b: October 19, 1879 in New York City, New York d: October 28, 1924 in Orange, Essex County, New Jersey
.... 2 Ernest Whitworth Marland b: May 08, 1874 in Pittsburgh, Allegheny County, Pennsylvania d: October 03, 1941 in Ponca City, Kay County, Oklahoma
.... +Mary Virginia Collins b: July 07, 1876 in Philadelphia, Pennsylvania d: June 06, 1926 in Ponca City, Kay County, Oklahoma
.... *2nd Wife of Ernest Whitworth Marland:
.... +Lydie Miller Roberts b: April 07, 1900 in Philadelphia, Philadelphia, Pennsylvania d: July 27, 1987 in Ponca City, Kay County, Oklahoma
.... 2 Alfred Marland, Jr. b: January 1877 in Pittsburgh, Allegheny County, Pennsylvania d: July 19, 1877 in Pittsburgh, Allegheny County, Pennsylvania

Marland Mansion
Time Line

May 8, 1874	Ernest Whitworth Marland born in Pittsburgh, Pennsylvania
1891	E.W. graduated from University of Michigan Law School
1903	E.W. married Mary Virginia Collins.
1907	E.W. lost first oil fortune in West Virginia.
1908	E.W. came to Ponca City, Oklahoma, looking for oil.
1911	Struck oil in Oklahoma for first time at Willie Cry well.
1916	E.W. built first mansion at 1000 East Grand in Ponca City. He and Virginia adopted George and Lydie Roberts.
1926	Mary Virginia Marland died.
1925-1928	E.W. built Marland Mansion at a cost of $5.5 million.
July 14, 1927	E.W. and Lydie Roberts were married at Flourtown, Pennsylvania.
September, 1928	E.W. and Lydie moved into the Marland Mansion.
November 1, 1929	E.W. resigned as president of Marland Oil Company.
April 22, 1930	Dedication of Pioneer Woman Statue.
1933-1934	E.W. serves in the United States House of Representatives.
1935-1939	E.W. serves as Oklahoma's tenth governor.
April, 1941	The mansion was sold to the Discalced Carmelite Fathers for $66,000.
October 7, 1941	E.W. Marland died.
1948	Mansion purchased by Felician Sisters for $50,000.
1953	Lydie Marland left Ponca City.
1957	George Marland died.
September, 1975	Lydie Marland returned to Ponca City.
September, 1975	City of Ponca City purchased Marland Mansion for $1,435,000.
July 27, 1987	Lydie Marland died.

Mayors of Ponca City

SINCE ACQUISITION OF THE MARLAND MANSION IN 1975

Kenneth E. Holmes 1974-1977

John R. Robinson 1977-1980

John W. Raley, Jr. 1980-1983

E. Lee Brown 1983-1986

Carl Balcer 1986-1992

Marilyn Andrews 1992-1998

Tom Leonard 1998-2004

Richard Stone 2004-

Directors

Charles Hepler *(cultural affairs director)* 1975-1984

Chuck Lessert *(assistant to Hepler)* 1978-1981

Rick Miller *(cultural affairs director)* 1984-1987

Paula Slater Winkleman *(acting director)* 1987-1988

John Sutton *(cultural affairs director)* 1988-1992

Patty Robinson Apman *(cultural affairs director)*   1993-1995

Kathy Adams *(Marland Estate director)* 1996-2002

David Keathly *(Marland Estate executive director)*   2002-

BELOW: The Marland Estate Commission in 2005. Left to right, front row, Gerald Nield, Becky Hatton, Natalie Lindsay, Mary Beth Glass, and Norma Beasley. Second row, Joe Hoyle, Sylvia Burns, Becky Poet, Marlene Foxworthy, and Don Gray. Back row, Pete James, Mike Phenix, Lana Jones, Sue Ziegenhain, Tamee Re'Peresko, and David Keathly. Not available for the photograph were Troy Lewis, Ford Lasher, and Shirley Jones.

ABOVE: Members of the Marland Estate Foundation board of directors in 2005. Left to right, front row, Louise Abercrombie, Sue Ziegenhain, Carolyn Renfro, Kathy Paczkowski, and Shirley Jones. Middle, Pat Evans. Back row, Larry Stephenson, Gene Thomas, Jack Branstetter, Tom Muchmore, Gary Bracken, and Dick Stone. Not available for the photograph were Martha Griffin, Steve Linville, John Brooks Walton, and Richard Winterrowd.

Bibliography
and Suggested Reading

Apman, Patti. *Lyde Roberts Marland, the Princess of the Palace on the Prairie.* Ponca City: Marland Mansion, 1995.

Baird, W. David and Danney Goble. *The Story of Oklahoma.* Norman: University of Oklahoma Press, 1994.

Burke, Bob. *Oklahoma: The Center of It All.* Encino, California: Cherbo Publishing Group, 2002.

Carlile, Glenda. *Petticoats, Politics, and Pirouette.* Oklahoma City: Southern Hills Publishing Company, 1995.

Crow, Betty and Bob Burke. *A History of the Oklahoma Governor's Mansion.* Oklahoma City: Oklahoma Heritage Association, 2004.

Fischer, Leroy H., ed. *Oklahoma's Governors 1929-1955: Depression to Prosperity,* Oklahoma City: Oklahoma Historical Society, 1983.

Franks, Kenny A., Paul Lambert, and Carl N. Tyson. *Early Oklahoma Oil.* College Station: Texas A & M Press, 1981.

Mathews, John Joseph. *E.W. Marland: Life and Death of an Oil Man.* Norman: University of Oklahoma Press, 1951.

Wade, Henry F. *Ship of State on a Sea of Oil.* Oklahoma City: privately printed, 1972.

Acknowledgments

THROUGHOUT THE LAST CENTURY, as the intriguing story of the Marland family unfolded, many people tried to preserve the history. Overzealous magazine writers and headline-seeking newspaper reporters took tiny bits of truth and turned them into full-blown, whimsical tales. After awhile, readers had no idea what to believe.

Feeling the need to preserve for future generations the factual account of E.W. Marland's arrival in Ponca City, his rise and fall in business and politics, and his unusual family relationships, we embarked upon this project.

This book is more than a gallery of photographs to display the magnificent Marland Mansion. It is a truthful account of the contributions, eccentricities, happy times, and sad times of the Marland family.

We are thankful to many people, including proofreaders, Robert E. "Bob" Clark, Jr., Sue Ziegenhain, Justice Steven Taylor, Judge Tom Leonard, Judge Mary Black, Reverend Kalyn and Lori Brassfield, and George and Marcia Davis. Bob Clark, whose mother was a dear childhood friend of Lydie Marland, was especially helpful in relating first hand knowledge of Lydie and E.W. Marland. Bob's careful critique of the manuscript was invaluable.

The current Marland Estate staff aided the effort tremendously. Director David Keathly, Connie Pruitt, Alice Holmes, and James Allensworth promptly answered every call for help.

The *Ponca City News* played a major role in the production of the book. Publisher Tom Muchmore led the fund raising effort for design and printing. Louise Abercrombie, who has chronicled the Marland family story for decades, gave much insight into the history of the family and mansion. Rick Logan provided old and new photographs. Photographs also came from the archives of the Oklahoma Publishing Company with the able assistance of Linda Lynn, Melissa Hayer, Mary Phillips, Robin Davison, and Billie Harry.

We also are indebted to Gene Thomas, Marci Gracey, Jerry Helms, James Thompson, Dustin Crawford, Lois Corbin, Richard Myers, and Tracy Hill for their assistance in the project.

—THE AUTHORS

Index

101 Ranch 23-29
101 Ranch Oil Company 32, 35, 43
101 Wild West Show 25

Abercrombie, Louise 183
Alcorn, John 70, 74, 83, 85
Allen, Curtis 76
American Legion Children's Home 43
American Legion Home School 50
Anglin, Tom 89
Arcade Hotel 26-30, 33, 38
Arkansas City, KS 107
Arkansas River 32, 42, 53
Arnold School 15
Ashton-Under-Line, England 9
Assumption Villa 129
Atlantic City, NJ 69
Autin, Fritz 53

Baker, Bryant 68, 73-74, 151
Barnes Hall 29
Barnes, B.S. 25
Barrington, Dee 122
Bartlesville, OK 29, 68, 115-116
Beasley, Norma 182
Berglund, Conrad 67
Betow, Wanda 122
Bigham, Kirk Q. 17
Billings field 35
Blackard, G.W. 85
Blackard, Grover 110
Blackard, Ruth 110
Blackwell, OK 35
Blauvelt, Howard W. 121
Boggess, Peg 59
Boggess, Tot 59
Bois d'Arc Creek 32
Boston, MA 56
Boyson, Harold 58
Brace, Jerry 122
Bracken, Gary 183
Braman field 35
Branstetter, Jack 183
Brazier, Claude 122
Briggs, Claud 91
British American Oil Producing Company 99
Broaddus, Annie Lee 57
Brookings Institution 93
Brown, Charles C. 51, 83, 86 building
Burns, Sylvia 182

Carnegie, Andrew 16
Carpenter, John 122
Carter, Jimmy 6
Carter, Lillian 6
Cassel, Louis 106-107
Cherokee Outlet 24
Cherokee Strip 68, 88
Chilocco Indian School 35
Churchill, Winston 151
City National Bank and Trust Company 109
Civil War 9
Claremore, OK 61
Clark, Dillard 70
Clark, Glen 53
Clark, Jane 104
Clark, Robert E., Jr. 24, 29, 69, 99-100, 105
Clark, Robert E., Sr. 38, 101, 108, 110
Clark, Ruth McDowell 38, 55-57, 59, 99
Cleary, Connie 110
Cleary, Helen 110
Cleary, Jack 70, 83, 91
Clinton, Bill 6
Collins, Lydie Miller 18
Collins, Samuel 18
Collins, Samuel, Jr. 19-20, 99
Comar Oil Company 45
Congo field 19, 21
Continental Oil Company 84-85, 117-120, 124-125
Cosden, Josh 45
Crawford, Foy 74, 76
Crimean War 9
Cruce, Lee 36
Cumberland Mountains 15

Davidson, Jo 67-68, 135, 148
Denver, CO 84
Deterding, Sir Henri 51
Detten, Jayne 7, 84, 145
Devers, Jacob 74
Discalced Carmelite Fathers 103
Donahoe, Dee 59
Donahoe, Edward 59
Duggins, Ron 122
Duvall, Felix 123

East Liverpool, OH 19
Eaton, John 23
Estes Park, CO 64
Evans, Pat 183

Federal Bureau of Investigation 108
Felician Sisters 106-107, 110, 118
Ferguson, Phil C. 87
First Baptist Church 29
First Presbyterian Chuch 124
Flourtown, PA 39, 77
Forsyth, John Duncan 61-64, 68
Foxworthy, Marlene 182
Frankoma Oil Company 45
French, Billie 122
Frick, Henry Clay 16
Frothingham, William 56, 59

Galey, John H. 17
Garber field 35
Garber, Milton C. 87
Gates, Ken 124
Gay, George 74
Geyer, F. Park 50
Gilchrist, Glen 105
Glass, Mary Beth 182
Glenn Pool 23, 29
Gore, Thomas P. 101
Gray, Don 182
Great Depression 84-85, 87-89, 101
Green Country Inn 114-115
Griffin, Martha 183

Guaranty Trust Company 80
Guffey, James M. 17
Gulf of Mexico 82

Hale, Corelia 104
Hale, John 51, 85, 88, 99, 101
Hall, Marie 57
Hall, Mrs. George 74
Hampton, J.C. 106
Hanks, J.D. 84
Hapgood, Prentice 122
Hargraves, Bill 123
Hatashita, Henry 39, 42
Hatton, Becky 182
Heagy, Gene 122
Henderson, Donald L. 70, 74
Henry Hotel 21
Hepler, Charles 122
Hillcrest Country Club 115
Holland, Florence 124
Holland, Gordon 124
Holloway, William J. 87
Holmes, Kenneth 84, 121
Holmes, Yvonne 84
Hoover, Herbert 87
Hoover, J. Edgar 108
Hot Springs, AR 116
Hoyle, Joe 182
Hudson's Bay Marland Oil Company 45
Hughes, Sir Thomas 15-16
Hunter, Evelyn 122
Hyde, Herbert K. 101

Interstate Oil Compact Commission 97-99

J.P. Morgan and Company 79
James, Pete 182
Jens Marie Hotel 116-117
John Alcorn Oil Company 45
Jones, David 123
Jones, Lana 182
Jones, Marion 122
Jones, Shirley 182-183

Kansas City, MO 55, 109
Kay County Gas Company 35, 53
Keathly, David 182
Kennedy, John F. 151
Kenney, Franklin Rockefeller 10, 23-24, 33, 51
Kenney-Cleary Oil Company 45
Kentucky Derby 56
Kobler, John 108

Lackey, Bill 53
Lancashire, England 9
Lasher, Ford 182
Lean-Bear's-Ear 30
Lee, Josh 101, 103
Lew Wentz scholarships 33
Lewis, Troy 182
Light, G.W. 29
Lincoln, Abraham 151
Lindsay, Natalie 182
Linville, Steve 183
Los Angeles Basin 81
Lowrance, Press 30
Lyons, Lana 121, 123

Macon, MO 108
Madero, Francisco 51
Mamaroneck, NY 39
Maranyck, NY 38
Margliotti, Vincent 67, 136-137
Maris and Maris 105
Markham, Baird 83
Marland Industrial Institute 46
Marland Oil Company 43-87, 150
Marland Oil Company of Mexico 45
Marland Oil Museum 150
Marland Production Company 45
Marland Refining Company 44-45
Marland, Alfred 9-15, 21
Marland, Anne Whitworth 10
Marland, Charlotte Anne 12
Marland, Elizabeth 13
Marland, Ernest Whitworth, birth and early life, 9-18; early oil development, 19-33; building Marland Oil Company, 34-85; as governor of Oklahoma, 88-101
Marland, George 10
Marland, George Frederick Roberts 37-44, 53, 61-62, 74-76, 85, 101
Marland, Henry 13
Marland, Ignatia 12
Marland, James 13, 21
Marland, Laverne Donohue 61, 101, 106
Marland, Lydie Roberts, birth and childhood, 37-59; marriage to E.W. Marland, 69-77; first lady of Oklahoma, 88-101; disappearance, 107-116; return to Ponca City, 119-125
Marland, Mary Virginia Collins, birth and childhood, 18; marriage to E.W. Marland 19-65
Marland, Neely Nut and Bolt Company 12
Marland, Sarah McLeod 10, 12
Mathews, John Joseph 13, 24, 79, 93
McCaskey, J.C. 33
McCoy, Alex 85
McCracken, H.L. 85
McDonald, Sandy 42
McElroy, Thomas 104
McFadden, W.H. 30, 33, 74, 83, 87, 91
McGraw, J.J. 45
Mellon Bank 18
Mellon, Andrew 18
Mellon, Thomas 18
Miller, George 23, 29-30, 33, 45
Miller, Rick 124
Miller, Walter 53, 77
Miss Merrill's School 38
Mississippi River 82
Mix, Tom 70
Monticello College 38, 55
Monticello, IL 38
Moonlight Inn 107
Moran, D.J. 83-84
Morgan, J. Pierpont 15
Mott, Mike 7, 42, 84, 145
Mott, Nancy 41-42
Mrs. Spence's School for Girls 38
Muchmore, Allen 122
Muchmore, JoAnne 122
Muchmore, Tom 183
Mueller, Harold L. 90
Murray, William H. 89, 93
My Experience With a Money Trust 36, 81
Myers, Richard 11

Nelson, Gwen 56-57
New Deal 88-90, 97
New Haven, CT 39
New York, NY 107
Newkirk, OK 35
Nield, Gerald 182
Nigh, George 6
Nightingale, Florence 9
Northcutt, C.E. 74
Northcutt, Clarence D. 103, 106, 110-117, 121, 122-124
Northcutt, John 122

Oaksmere School 39
Oil Well Supply Company 23, 30
Oklahoma City Times 90
Oklahoma Highway Patrol 98
Oklahoma Military Academy 91
Oklahoma State Bureau of Investigation 107
Oklahoma State University 61, 122
Oliver, Earl 53
Omart, Dorothy 59
Osage Nation 24, 45
Osborn, Harold 58

Paczkowski, Kathy 183
Panton, Marjorie 57
Paris, Leslie 122
Park Institute 16
Patton, George 74
Peel, Madalynne 122
People's Fuel Supply Company 45
Permian Basin 82
Permian Red Beds 35
Peter-Knows-the-Country 30
Phenix, Mike 182
Philadelphia, PA 18-19
Phillips, Leon C. 91, 97
Pine, William B. 89

Pioneer Woman Statue 68-69, 73-74, 87
Pittsburgh Securities and Guaranty Company 18
Pittsburgh, PA 9-12
Plaza Hotel 39
Ponca City Chamber of Commerce 106
Ponca City News 62, 117
Ponca City Polo Association 70
Ponca Indian Reservation 24-25
Ponca Townsite Company 25
Post, Becky 182
Potter, W.C. 80, 82
Prather, Maxine 3
Prather, Paul 3, 104-105
Pryse, Dane L. 135
Pryse, Zack, Jr. 135

Radd, Fred 122
Raley, John 123
Re'Peresko, Tamee 182
Red Fork oil field 23, 29
Reed, Lyman 55
Regan County Purchasing Company 45

Renfro, Carolyn 122, 183
Richie, Jane 59
Rittenhouse, Louis 12
Roberts, Ernest Marland 37
Roberts, George Frederick 37
Roberts, George W. 37
Roberts, Margaret 37
Roberts, Marland 125
Roberts, Mary Virginia 37
Robinson, John 121
Rochedale Parish 9-10
Rockefeller, John D. 15
Rodman, Carroll 115
Rogers, Will 70, 74
Roosevelt, Franklin D. 88
Royal Dutch Shell Company 51
Rugby School 15-16
Running-After-Arrow 33

Salt Fork 32
Salvation Army 124
Santa Fe, NM 121
Sarchet, Rebecca 59
Saturday Evening Post 107-111
School Land Commission 35-36

Scott, Jessie 57
Seal Beach field 81
Security Bank 111, 116, 119
Shallenberger, George 53, 74, 76
Sheets, Nan 80
Sheldon, S.R. 83
Sisters of St. Joseph 50
Smithers, Charles F. 80
Smithsonian Institution 146
Soldani, Rose 57
Sophian, Abraham 55
Sperring, Anna Eliza 21
St. Louis, MO 117
St. Mary's High School 39
St. Thomas Church 77
Standard Oil Company 19, 35
Standing Bear 32
State Board of Education 104
Stephenson, Larry 119, 121-122, 124, 183
Stephenson, Virginia 119
Stillwater, OK 61
Stone, Dick 183
Thomas Cook and Son, Inc. 110

Thomas, Elmer 101
Thomas, Gene 124-125, 183
Thompson, Betty 121, 123
Thompson, Charles 121, 123
Three Sands field 35
Tom Brown's School Days 15
Tom James Oil Company 45
Tonkawa field 35
Tonkawa, OK 35
Truscott, Lucian 74
Tulsa World 116
Tulsa, OK 116
Turkey Foot oil field 18

University of Michigan 16
University of Oklahoma 53, 103

van Waterschoot, W.A.J.M. 51
Vaughan, F.L. 87
Villa, Pancho 51

Wainwright, Jonathan J. 74
Waldo, Gene 23, 43, 85, 99, 101
Walker, Carol 122
Walker, Don 57

Walton, John Brooks 183
Warren, Maxine 122
Washington, D.C. 67, 110-111, 115
Washington, PA 13
Webster High School 61
Wentz, Lew 33, 87
West Virginia Coal Company 18
Westfall, Chester 53
Westmoreland, Bob 122
White Eagle 32-33
Whitemarsh Lake 65, 99
Whitemarsh, PA 77
Whitney, George 18, 80
Whitworth School for Boys 9
Will Rogers Memorial 61
Willie-Crys-for-War 32-33
Winterrowd, Richard 183
Woolaroc Museum 68
World War I 56

Yale University 39
Young Men's Christian Association 43

Ziegenhahn, Sue 182-183